The Law
and the Lore of
Endowment Funds

The Educational Endowment Series

The Law
and the Lore of
Endowment Funds

REPORT TO THE FORD FOUNDATION

William L. Cary and Craig B. Bright

Library of Congress Catalog Card Number 77-83377
April 1969
Additional copies may be obtained by writing the
Ford Foundation, Office of Reports,
320 East 43rd Street, New York, N. Y. 10017.

Foreword

This study of the law governing the endowment funds of colleges and universities was prepared by Mr. William L. Cary of the New York firm of Patterson, Belknap & Webb, in association with Mr. Craig B. Bright of the same firm. This report is one of the products of a general study of endowment management supported by the Ford Foundation in the hope that new knowledge and informed commentary about charitable investments will strengthen the efforts of colleges and universities to improve their endowment income. While the findings and recommendations reported by Mr. Cary and Mr. Bright are their own, they have had the advice and comment of an advisory committee of lawyers distinguished for their understanding of the field of charitable corporations.

This report addresses questions of law on which the Ford Foundation as an institution takes no position. What we do believe is that this report is a serious contribution to public consideration of a subject which is critically important to the financial strength of American education, and that it deserves prompt publication. We are deeply indebted to Mr. Cary, Mr. Bright, and their advisers, and we hope their study may commend itself to the attention of trustees and legal counselors in the world of American higher learning.

McGeorge Bundy

March 28, 1969

Mr. McGeorge Bundy, President
The Ford Foundation
320 East 43rd Street
New York, N.Y. 10017

Dear Mr. Bundy:

We have examined the report entitled "The Law and the Lore of Endowment Funds," prepared by William L. Cary and Craig B. Bright under the sponsorship of the Ford Foundation. In our opinion this report offers a thoughtful diagnosis of the investment problems of educational institutions and a comprehensive examination of the degree to which those problems are created or aggravated by rules of law. We believe the conclusions and recommendations of the report deserve serious consideration by all who bear major responsibility for university investments.

Very truly yours,

ELI WHITNEY DEBEVOISE
New York, New York

LEWIS F. POWELL, JR.
Richmond, Virginia

MORRIS M. DOYLE
San Francisco, California

H. CHAPMAN ROSE
Cleveland, Ohio

PAUL HARBRECHT, S.J.
Washington, D.C.

AUSTIN WAKEMAN SCOTT
Cambridge, Massachusetts

STEPHEN H. HART
Denver, Colorado

FREDERICK SHEFFIELD
New York, New York

GLEN A. LLOYD
Chicago, Illinois

ALAN M. STROOCK
New York, New York

BETHUEL M. WEBSTER
New York, New York

Contents

The Law
and the Lore of
Endowment Funds

Genesis of the Report

In his first report as president of the Ford Foundation, McGeorge Bundy commented that room exists for great improvement in the investment performance of college and university endowment funds. This memorandum summarizes the results of one of several studies which had their genesis in Mr. Bundy's observation. We examine the law governing endowment funds in an attempt to determine its bearing on the formulation of a sound investment policy. Is the law a neutral factor, giving the directors of an educational institution freedom to formulate the investment policy best suited to meet its particular needs? Or does the law limit their flexibility and foreclose choices which would otherwise be open to them? Suggestions are made for improving the law itself, where that seems feasible, and for harnessing its most beneficial aspects through improved terminology in donative instruments covering gifts to endowment funds.

It seems impossible to overstress the importance of the nation's colleges and universities to the continued growth and even to the continued existence of our country. The problems of financing higher education may not be as dramatic as those involving the war on poverty or our role in Southeast Asia, but in long-term perspective their solution is scarcely less vital. Alfred North Whitehead stated the problem well half a century ago:

> "In the conditions of modern life the rule is absolute: The race which does not value trained intelligence is doomed. . . . Today we maintain ourselves. Tomorrow science will have moved forward yet one more step, and there will be no appeal from the judgment which will then be pronounced on the uneducated."[1]

The cost of financing higher education has grown tremendously since the Second World War and the rate of increase is accelerating.[2] The endowment funds of colleges and universities have increased, too, but not nearly as rapidly.[3] In 1900 the earnings of endowment funds paid 25% of the costs of higher education; by the late 1950s the relative

1

contribution of endowment earnings was only one-fifth as large, or 5%.[4]

Diminished though the role of endowment funds may be, they nevertheless remain vitally important to a number of institutions and their contribution to higher education in general remains indispensable.[5] Even for institutions with relatively small endowments, the earnings from invested funds sometimes provide the thin margin necessary to escape a deficit. College and university managers have been taxing their ingenuity for years in an effort to find and exploit to the fullest every conceivable source of revenue. If endowment funds were taken from them or if their contribution were seriously reduced, alternative sources in many cases would be simply unavailable. The inevitable result would be the curtailment of operations and a decline in the high level of the nation's educational standards. For this reason it is mandatory that every effort be made to preserve and if possible to increase the purchasing power of our endowment funds.

I
The Meaning of "Income"

While the explosive increase in costs has been the primary reason for the comparative decline in the importance of the contribution of endowment funds, it has not been the only reason. The portfolios of many endowment funds have been far too heavily laden with fixed-income securities to resist the relentless erosion of inflation. In a decade when the average price of common stocks has risen seven times as fast as the cost of living, and dividends on common stocks have risen three and a half times as fast,[6] many endowments have been exceedingly hard pressed even to keep abreast.

To some extent this has been the result of a conscious choice on the part of endowment fund managers. As a group they are conservative,[7] and some of them have insisted that their only duty is to safeguard the original dollar value of the funds entrusted to their care. Like the cautious servant in the parable of the talents, they have been well pleased to bury their funds, complacent in the belief that if their talents cannot multiply under their supervision at least they will not be lost.[8] But their talents have been lost, a little each year, as surely as if they were squandered or thrown away. Instead of safeguarding the legacy of tomorrow's students such managers have sacrificed it to fiscal "conservatism."

The great majority of endowment fund managers, however, are well aware that it is no longer "conservative" or prudent to ignore possibilities for long-term growth in formulating their investment policies.[9] In choosing between a high current yield of dividends and interest on the one hand, and long-term growth of principal on the other, they strive conscientiously·to strike a balance between the demands of today and those of tomorrow. But too often the desperate need of some institutions for funds to meet current operating expenses has led their managers, contrary to their best long-term judgment, to forego investments with favorable growth prospects if they have a low current yield.*

It has been suggested that it would be far wiser to take capital gains as well as dividends and interest into account in investing for the highest overall return consistent with the safety and preservation of the funds

---

*For purposes of this report we polled all institutions of higher learning in the United States with investment portfolios having a market value of $3,000,000 or more as of June 30, 1967. Approximately 300 institutions were questioned, of which 186 furnished information about their investment practices. Eighty-five per cent of the responding institutions stated that their choice of investments is influenced at least to some extent by a desire for a high current return of dividends and interest, and 11% stated that their choice is influenced to a great extent by that desire. Conversely, 67% stated that a low current return of dividends and interest sometimes dissuades them from making investments with "unusually attractive long-term growth prospects." For 8% of the institutions a low current return is usually sufficient to block such an investment.

invested. If the current return is insufficient for the institution's needs, the difference between that return and what it would have been under a more restrictive policy can be made up by the use of a prudent portion of capital gains. This suggestion has repeatedly been met with the response that as a matter of law the capital gains of endowment funds may not be expended, because the principal of endowment funds must be maintained intact and in perpetuity and capital gains are part of that principal.*

The sections of this report which immediately follow are devoted in large measure to an analysis of the validity and effects of that response.

Moral Issues

It should be stressed at the outset that the purpose of this report is not to advocate either the expenditure or the preservation of capital gains. We do not presume to chart the "proper course" for all institutions, regardless of circumstances. The object of our inquiry is merely to determine whether the directors of an educational institution are circumscribed by the law or are free to adopt the investment policy they regard as soundest for their institution, unhampered by legal impediments, prohibitions or restrictions.

There is strong and vehement objection in some academic circles to any discussion of the proper allocation to principal or income of the realized gains of endowment funds, because for some persons the issue is a moral or ethical one which is not open to reasoned debate. Such persons argue that educational institutions are charged with the duty and responsibility of maintaining the principal of their endowment inviolate, and that principal "necessarily" includes realized appreciation. Many of them fail or are unwilling to recognize the latter part of that

---

*Of the institutions which responded to the questionnaire described in the preceding footnote, 50% stated that their investment portfolios would be changed to include more growth stocks if they were legally free to spend the capital gains of their endowment funds. Ten per cent of the institutions would purchase many more such stocks.

6

argument as nothing more than an assumption, the validity of which may be questioned. As was noted at a seminar on the financial problems of higher education:

> "We may be in a period in which the mores regarding these matters are gradually shifting. Fifty years ago most trustees would have argued that it was immoral to purchase common stocks with endowment funds. At present nearly half of college endowment funds are in common stocks, and a similar shift with respect to [the utilization of] capital gains may be occurring."[10]

It should be clear to any legal scholar that there is nothing inherently sacrosanct about traditional views of principal and income, even as they apply to private trusts. Many of the views which are prevalent today in the trust field became so quite recently, after many years of debate between proponents of a number of competing treatments, and there is no evidence that the evolutionary process has ceased. It should be remembered that the strength of our system of jurisprudence has historically been its ability to adapt and change in response to the evolving needs of society. As the Supreme Court of Pennsylvania said in a recent case:

> "Due process does not mandate that prior decisions or rules remain effective and controlling forever. Thus, it is settled that there is no vested interest in a definition or method of ascertaining income."[11]

There are those who insist that capital gains of endowment funds must be treated as principal, whether or not the law requires such treatment. They argue that any other treatment would thwart the intent of the donors of the funds.[12] But as Professor Scott has observed in this connection:

> "The great difficulty with any argument based upon the intention of the settlor is that he generally fails to state his intention. The reason why he does not do so may be and generally is that the question never occurs to him. Ordinarily, therefore, the question is not what he intended or probably intended but what he would probably have intended if he had ever considered the matter. All that can be said with any confidence is that he would have intended whatever is fair and just, and we have already seen how difficult it is to determine what is fair and just. . . ."[13]*

---

*As we point out later, donors very seldom give the slightest indication of how they want the capital gains of their gifts to be treated. Further, judicial interpretations of the presumed intent of donors in this respect are almost non-existent. An example is a decision of the Orphan's Court in Pennsylvania, which was asked to interpret a testamentary trust which required "interest and income" to be paid to named charities in perpetuity. The court held that the donor had intended "income" to include both realized and unrealized appreciation.

Even if the donor had intended one accounting treatment in a given set of circumstances, would it be reasonable to assume that he intended that treatment to be applied through all eternity, regardless of changes in the financial and investment community? John Stuart Mill commented on such a position some time ago:

> "Under the guise of fulfilling a bequest, this is making a dead man's intentions for a single day a rule for subsequent centuries, when we know not whether he himself would have made it a rule even for the morrow. . . . No reasonable man, who gave his money, when living, for the benefit of the community, would have desired that his mode of benefiting the community should be adhered to when a better could be found."[15]

Proponents of the theory that capital gains must be treated as principal, regardless of the requirements of the law, argue that failure to follow their mandate will lead to a decline in gifts to charity, because donors can no longer rely on their wishes being enforced.[16] Again, this argument is based on the questionable assumption that those wishes have been properly interpreted by the proponents of the argument. But even if it were granted, *arguendo,* that the intent of donors in this matter of administration could accurately be divined, the words of Professor Scott from half a century ago in his article entitled "Education and the Dead Hand" seem apropos:

> "It may be suggested that unless donors can rely upon the strict observance of all their directions they will be dissuaded from making gifts for charitable purposes. But experience in England shows the fact to be otherwise. Charitable gifts were never more common in England than in the early days of the Reformation, when the fact that Henry VIII had defeated the intentions of many a founder of religious institutions was fresh in the minds of every Englishman. Bequests to the English universities actually increased after Parliament had authorized them to depart from the directions of their founders and benefactors. It would seem rather that the charitably minded would be discouraged by the sight of charitable institutions gradually ceasing to accomplish the high purposes for which they were created."[17]

Otherwise such gains would be accumulated to pass eventually to charities completely unknown to the testator, through the application of the doctrine of cy pres, upon the dissolution of the charities he intended to favor.[14]

We have found no case in which a court was asked to determine whether the capital gains of the endowment funds of a charitable corporation, held by the corporation itself, should be classified as principal or as income.

Colleges and universities obtain the money to pay their bills from a variety of sources, such as tuition, governmental grants and private gifts. Gifts may be unrestricted, in the sense that they may be fully expended at any time in the discretion of the institution, or they may be intended to form part of the institution's endowment, which has been defined in the landmark decision in this field, *St. Joseph's Hosp. v. Bennett,* 281 N. Y. 115, 118, 22 N. E. 2d 305, 306 (1939), as "the bestowment of money as a permanent fund, the income of which is to be used in the administration of a proposed work." It is endowment and the income therefrom with which we are concerned. Further, we are here focusing only upon endowment funds held and administered by the institution itself for its own purposes, not with funds held in trust by some third party for the benefit of the institution, and not with funds held by the institution for the benefit of some third party.*

To determine the duties and responsibilities of an institution of higher learning in the administration of its collective endowment funds, one must start with the restrictions and conditions imposed by the donors of the individual funds which comprise the collective endowment. For this purpose we examined all donative instruments relating to the largest individual funds** held by each of a cross-section of private institutions in the East, together with a random sampling of donative instruments relating to smaller individual funds.*** In all the analysis covered 462 instruments governing individual funds with an

---

*A number of institutions hold funds the income of which they have agreed to pay to the donor during his lifetime or for a specified number of years. Such funds are the substantial equivalent of private trusts, with the institution's interest limited to that of a remainderman. Because of their special nature it may be necessary to invest such funds separately from other funds held by the institution, and to use a different measure to compute their income.

**The individual funds chosen were all those with a current market value in excess of $100,000, $400,000 or $500,000, depending upon the size of the institution's entire endowment.

***The smaller funds averaged $40,000 to $50,000 in size.

aggregate market value of over half a billion dollars. No significant differences were discovered between larger and smaller individual funds or from institution to institution in respect of the matters discussed below.

Instruments Not Germane to our Study: Approximately 30% of the instruments we reviewed turned out to be irrelevant to the issue now before us. We restricted our study to funds which the institutions classified as "pure endowment"; that is, those funds the principal of which the institutions considered themselves to be legally barred from spending. Nevertheless, we discovered that approximately 22% of the instruments studied (both in number of instruments and dollar amount of the funds involved) contained no legal prohibition whatsoever against spending principal. Many explicitly authorized the institutions to expend principal in their discretion. This suggests that at least some of the restrictions which supposedly fetter the free exercise of discretion in this area are wholly imaginary, arising from misclassification. It also indicates that any institution concerned about the problem would be well advised to have its attorneys make a careful study of its donative instruments.

A small number of instruments (covering approximately 5% of the aggregate value of the funds studied) employed formal trust language in describing the grant. This circumstance makes it somewhat more likely that a court would apply trust principles in determining the standards which govern the administration of the fund, although the weight given to such language clearly varies from jurisdiction to jurisdiction and from instrument to instrument. For simplicity this memorandum will deal with the great majority of instruments, those which contain no trust language.

In only seven of the instruments studied, covering less than 1% of the aggregate value of the funds involved, did the donor give any indication of how he wished capital gains to be treated. In five of these the donor specified that capital gains may be expended currently, as income. The remaining two instruments treated the matter only tangentially, and their meaning is obscure. In five additional instruments, covering between 1% and 2% of the aggregate value of the funds involved, the donor specified that a definite sum of money from the donated fund was to be devoted to a specified purpose each year, regardless of whether the "earnings" of the fund were more or less than that amount. Such instruments are not concerned with income or principal as such. Income and capital gains and principal would all be expendable to the extent needed to meet the specified amount each year.

For the reasons stated we put aside all of the foregoing instruments, which together account for 30% of the aggregate value of the funds studied, and turn our attention to the remainder. In these remaining instruments, whether or not explicit directions are set forth as to the retention or expenditure of principal and income, there is no indication, whether explicit or obscure, of the donor's intent in respect of capital gains. These are the instruments with which we are concerned, where the donor's intent has not been made clear.

Instruments Germane to Our Study: From the remaining balance of 70%, a small group of instruments, covering about 8% of the aggregate value of the funds studied, explicitly direct that principal is to be kept intact or that only the income is to be spent. A few of those which refer to principal make it clear that the donor had in mind only the original dollar value of his gift. The remainder give no indication as to whether the donor considered principal to include or exclude realized or unrealized appreciation.

Instruments covering approximately 35% of the aggregate value of the funds studied (or about half of the aggregate value of the funds we consider germane) employed the word "endowment," and approximately one-third of these went on to give instructions as to the use of income. As was stated earlier, endowment has been judicially defined as "the bestowment of money as a permanent fund, the income of which is to be used in the administration of a proposed work."[18]

The remaining instruments, covering approximately 27% of the aggregate value of the funds studied, merely contain directions about the use of income or describe the gifts as a "permanent fund" or a "contribution to capital." While none of these uses the word "endowment" or specifies that principal is to be maintained intact, the inference could fairly be drawn that the donor did have in mind the investment of the principal and the expenditure only of the income therefrom, whatever that might be.

To summarize, the most restrictive prohibition against the expenditure of principal which is contained in any of the instruments in this group would read somewhat as follows:

> "This fund is given to X University with the direction and upon the understanding that the principal of the fund is to be maintained inviolate and in perpetuity, and that only the income from the investments of the funds may be expended."

11

Most of the instruments studied are not nearly so restrictive. Therefore, with the minor exception of formal trust instruments, an analysis of such words would cover the most stringent donor-imposed restrictions on spending principal of all the endowment funds studied.*

The Question Presented

If only income can be expended and principal must be maintained inviolate, there remains the question whether realized appreciation constitutes income or principal. As already stated, we have found no case in which this question has been answered or even posed in respect of endowment funds held by charitable corporations.

The only state which has a statute specifically dealing with the problem is Indiana, which forbids institutions of higher learning to pay current expenses with property which they receive for endowment, but permits them to use "the increase, rents, interests or profits" of such property for that purpose.[19] The quoted language seems broad enough to include realized appreciation, but we have found no case which holds that it does so.**

New Jersey does not deal with the problem specifically, but its principal and income act allocates capital gains to principal, and the unique

---

*This conclusion is subject to one caveat. Approximately 1½% of the instruments studied (in terms of dollar value of the covered funds) contained explicit instructions to maintain the principal intact, and went on to provide that if principal is impaired by losses or depreciation the deficit is to be made up by accumulating future income. It seems clear that such an instruction can have meaning only if "principal" is defined in terms of the original dollar value, or "book value," of the gift. If such a deficit arose, the use of income and gains on any part of the covered portfolio (whether or not gains are considered "income") would be restricted until the deficit was repaired.

**New York's Joint Legislative Committee to Study Revision of Corporation Laws recommended in January 1969 adoption of a bill which would include in the income of the endowment funds of charitable corporations "so much of the appreciation of principal as the board [of directors of the corporation] may deem prudent." S. 956, A. 1690 § 513(d) (N.Y. 1969-1970). The bill would apply to not-for-profit corporations generally but not to most educational institutions, in the absence of supplementary legislation. A revised form of the bill, introduced in March 1969, would require appreciation to be realized before it could be included in income. S. 956A (N.Y. 1969-1970).

definition of "fiduciary" in the act is broad enough to include charitable corporations.[20] Again, no case has been found which so holds.

Although with the possible exceptions of Indiana and New Jersey the law has not yet directed charitable corporations how to treat their capital gains, it has done so for other institutions and relationships. In the case of private trusts, where the trustee must make a fair division of trust revenue between the income beneficiary and the remainderman (two distinct and antagonistic interests), capital gains are generally considered part of principal, to be retained for the remainderman.* This is the position taken in both the original and revised versions of the Uniform Principal and Income Acts, one or the other of which has now been adopted in a majority of states. But these acts have no direct application to the endowment funds of charitable corporations, or even to perpetual trusts for charity,[27] since they deal with situations where principal is "eventually to be delivered to a remainderman while the return or use of the principal is in the meantime taken or received by or held for accumulation for an income beneficiary."** In our situation not only the income beneficiary and the remainderman but even the "trustee" are one and the same; principal is not to be maintained intact for delivery in the future, but instead is already held by the remainderman.***

---

*This is not uniformly true. Where a trustee holds shares of regulated investment companies which make capital gains distributions, a number of states allocate the distributions to income.[21] New York, which had been the leader in this regard, recently changed its rule by statute.[22]

A similar example of deviations from the stated rule is an outgrowth of the controversy over the proper allocation of extraordinary corporate dividends. At one time the great majority of jurisdictions followed the Pennsylvania rule, which allocates to the income beneficiary the proceeds of such dividends to the extent they are attributable to earnings of the corporation involved which have been accumulated but undistributed during the time the shares are held by the trustee.[23] Several states including Pennsylvania carried this principle to its logical conclusion by requiring a similar division of capital gains realized by the trustee on sale of the shares.[24] Some states including Pennsylvania have now switched to the competing Massachusetts rule, which allocates all cash dividends to income and all stock dividends to principal. That the Pennsylvania rule is fairer seems undisputed; the Massachusetts rule, where it has been adopted, has been favored for its simplicity of application.[25]

When the sale of unproductive or substantially underproductive property held in trust is delayed after a duty to sell arises, a portion of the proceeds of sale when they are realized is generally given to the income beneficiary to make up for his lost income.[26]

**The quotation is from the Revised Uniform Principal and Income Act. The original act in this respect is substantially the same.

Pennsylvania modified the original act by including in "principal" property which is "to remain in trust indefinitely." PA. STAT. ANN. tit. 20, § 3470.1 (1947). If a charitable corporation were considered in Pennsylvania to hold its property in trust, an argument could thus be made that the act applies to such a corporation. No case has been found in which such an argument was advanced.

Louisiana reworded the Revised Uniform Principal and Income Act in order to adapt it to the civil law system, and in the process eliminated references to a remainderman. LA. REV. STAT. ANN. § 9:2144 (1964). The distinction spelled out in text therefore does not apply, and the argument could thus be made that the Act applies to charitable corporations. Once again, no case has been found in which such an argument was made.

***Judge Charles E. Clark, the principal draftsman of the original act, in explaining why the act did not purport to establish rules for principal and income allocations of perpetual trusts, said that this was "a question of the most profound public importance but hardly to be solved

In the case of business corporations, where there is no dichotomy between the income beneficiary and the remainderman, capital gains are profits (income) and not part of capital (principal). This will be discussed more fully later in this report,* but for the present it is sufficient merely to note that an application of the principles of corporate law would lead one to a conclusion directly opposite from the one which would be reached by applying trust principles.

In the absence of a specific directive by the law on the proper allocation of realized appreciation of endowment funds, we next turn for guidance to an examination of the law governing charitable corporations in general. And in view of the divergence of trust law and corporate law on the point, we shall examine with special care the situations under which the courts apply corporate principles on the one hand or trust principles on the other to the solution of problems relating to charitable corporations.

The Law in General: A Battle of Semantics

The law relating to charitable corporations in general, and particularly to the administration of endowment funds, remains throughout the nation both "rudimentary and vague."[29] "[T]he great and rapid increase in the number and aggregate wealth of charitable corporations has taken the law by surprise,"[30] and the courts and commentators are still groping for a solution.

without extensive study of its social implications."[28]

Professor Allison Dunham, Executive Director of the National Conference of Commissioners on Uniform State Laws and the principal draftsman of the revised act, informs us that the draftsmen of that act also intended it to apply only to the income beneficiary and remainder-man relationship of normal trusts. They did not even discuss the rules applicable to charitable corporations or perpetual trusts for charities.

*See pp. 27-28, *infra.*

A charitable corporation is obviously similar to other corporations. It also shares certain characteristics with charitable trusts, and the agreements it reaches with the donors of its endowment funds are in the nature of contracts. The separate principles evolved by the law in relation to corporations, trusts and contracts are all quite well developed, and the courts and commentators have naturally drawn upon those principles in attempting to determine what standards should govern the administration of endowment funds. Unfortunately those principles are not always complementary; at times they are in direct conflict. The result has been "an uneasy mixture of trust, contract and corporation language, the force of which may be difficult to predict in a particular situation."[31] The debate has often centered on the label to be applied, rather than on an analysis of the principles involved; too often, the selection of the label has determined the result.[32] At other times the label has been used as a convenient rationalization of a socially desirable result, again without analysis of the principles.

Although the exercise is not overly helpful, American jurisdictions can be classified as falling into one of three broad categories, depending upon the view they take of the capacity in which educational institutions hold their endowment funds. It should be noted that such a classification can make no claim to being precise. The views of any given court as to applicable principles will vary in light of the issues before it, and cases can therefore be found which by themselves would place any jurisdiction in all three of the following categories. That is the principal reason the classification is not particularly helpful.

The Doctrine of Absolute Ownership: The first category, of which New York is the exemplar, consists of jurisdictions which hold that educational institutions are the absolute owners of their endowment funds.[33] Even specific words of trust in donative instruments are often brushed aside in these jurisdictions as excess verbiage.[34] All formal trusts involve a separation of the legal and equitable titles to the trust property, and no person can be trustee for himself; therefore, courts in these jurisdictions say, it follows that educational institutions cannot be trustees of their own endowment funds.[35]

Some but not all of the jurisdictions in this first category adopted the theory of absolute ownership as a means of saving gifts to charity which would otherwise have been struck down because of the invalidity of most charitable trusts.* If such gifts were construed as absolute and not in

---

*Because of the social disadvantages of allowing the "dead hand of the past" to control for too long the disposition of property, it has for centuries been a tenet of Anglo-Saxon juris-

15

trust, it was possible to sustain them. Such construction eventually became a rule of law, and by the end of the 19th century the Court of Appeals in New York used the following language in reversing a lower court which had invalidated a charitable bequest through the blind application of trust principles:

> "The fundamental error in this case . . . is the failure to recognize the fact that gifts to religious and charitable corporations to aid in carrying out the purposes for which they are organized, whether by expending the principal of a bequest, or the income of a bequest to be invested in perpetuity, do not create a trust in any legal sense, do not offend against the statutes of perpetuities, are not to be judged by any of the well-known rules pertaining to the law of trusts as applied to private individuals."[38]

The reasoning employed in such cases was persuasive enough to lead to the adoption of the doctrine of absolute ownership even in jurisdictions where charitable trusts have always been enforced.[93] And, even though the charitable trust exception to the basic tenets of trust law has now been restored by statute or judicial decision in all of the states which repealed the Statute of 43 Elizabeth I,[40] the doctrine of absolute ownership continues to be today a viable part of their judicial fabric.

The Trust Theory: The second category of jurisdictions consists of those which hold that all gifts to charitable corporations are made in trust, whether or not the donor employs trust language in making the grant, or restricts the purpose for which it can be used, or requires the principal to be maintained intact. When courts in such jurisdictions are confronted with the argument that a trust must entail the separation of the legal and equitable titles to the trust property, and that therefore no college can hold property in trust for itself, they rationalize their position by stating that the college holds its property in trust not for itself but for its students or for the public at large.[41] New Jersey is the exemplar of the states in this category.[42]

---

prudence that trusts will not be enforced unless they terminate within a reasonable period of time (usually a period measured by lives in being at the time the trust is created, plus 21 years). Further, the beneficiaries of the trust must be clearly ascertainable. During the fifteenth century an exception to these tenets developed in the practice of English courts of chancery for the benefit of charitable trusts, and in 1601 the exception received a semblance of legislative support with the passage of the Statute of 43 Elizabeth I, ch. 4.

After the American Revolution a number of states repealed all English statutes en masse, including (without specification) the Statute of 43 Elizabeth I. Overlooking the practice which had developed in the courts of chancery at an early stage, quite independent of the subsequent legislation, some courts reasoned that the repeal of the statute had destroyed the exception to the general tenets described above, with the result that charitable trusts for indefinite periods or for indefinite beneficiaries could no longer be enforced.[36]

In New York, Michigan, Wisconsin and Minnesota, an additional reason for the invalidation of charitable trusts was the adoption of statutes abolishing all but four types of trusts. Charitable trusts as such did not fall within any of the four exceptions.[37]

In considering this classification it should be borne in mind that "trust" is a word with many meanings, and it is frequently quite difficult to tell just what a court means when it says that a charitable corporation holds its property in trust. It may be describing a technical, legal trusteeship, or it may merely be observing that charitable corporations occupy a position of public confidence and responsibility. The difference was recognized by a California court, in commenting on an argument that certain property was held by a municipality in trust:

> "Admittedly this beach property may be loosely referred to as a 'public trust' for the residents of Hermosa Beach, but such a public trust is no more a true charitable trust than was Grover Cleveland's in his expression 'a public office is a public trust.' "[43]

A Louisiana court met a similar argument with the following observation:

> "The word 'trust' as it is used in the argument on behalf of the city means . . . a full and complete ownership coupled with a moral obligation to use in accordance with the wishes and instructions of the donor—the testator. And, of course, no one will for a moment deny that in that sense the McDonough will provided for legacies 'in trust' to the legatee cities. That kind of trust is the one referred to in the familiar statement often cited but unfortunately often not honored in the observance: 'A public office is a public trust.' That is the kind of trust which is here involved in the title of the City of New Orleans, and it does not affect the legal title but only the obligation which is imposed by the ownership of title—the moral obligation to see that the property is devoted to the education of the youth of the area."[44]

The Donor's Intent: The third category of states is composed of those which hold that an educational institution can be either the absolute owner of its endowment funds or the trustee thereof, depending upon the terms imposed by the donors of the funds in making their donations. Massachusetts is an example.[45] A number of these states could also be listed as proponents of the doctrine of absolute ownership, in that they require quite explicit directions from the donor before finding that a gift is held in trust and not absolutely. The difference between such states and states in the first category is at most one of shading.

It should also be noted that the courts in all jurisdictions pay at least lip service to the necessity of observing the donor's intent. In practice the attempt to ascertain that intent is often an exercise in futility, which ultimately ends with the predilections of the court masquerading as the wishes of a deceased donor who is no longer able to speak for himself.

The observation of Professor Scott in this regard should be recalled.*

To summarize, despite the rough classification which has been spelled out above, in none of the states do the courts look only to trust principles, or only to corporate principles, or only to contract principles, for the solution of problems relating to the funds of charitable corporations. An examination of the cases makes it clear that the choice of principles depends upon the factual situation presented and upon the result which the courts deem it socially desirable to attain. With this in mind we have attempted in the next two sections to group the cases according to the problems presented and the results attained. Since we are concerned with the administration of endowment funds, all cases specifically dealing with administration and housekeeping will be treated separately.

We deal first in summary fashion with cases not involving administration as such. A more detailed analysis appears in an appendix to this report.

Cases
Not Involving
Administration

In many of these cases a charitable corporation and some other claimant vie for possession of a fund, or the title of the charitable corporation to its property is otherwise put in question. The courts in all jurisdictions go to great lengths to preserve the property for charity. Trust principles or corporate principles are applied if they happen to be of assistance in reaching the desired conclusion, and no undue concern is shown for the niceties of logic and consistency in choosing between the two.**

---

*See p. 7, *supra.*

**Of course this is not to say that courts invariably hold in favor of the charity, regardless of the circumstances. Cases can be found where the charity lost because the nature of its property interest was absolute and not in trust,[46] or in trust and not absolute.[47] The point is that such holdings are comparatively rare.

Where monetary considerations are not involved, however, the picture is less clear. In most such cases the choice of trust principles or corporate principles is neither determinative of the result nor particularly useful in rationalizing it, and the passing references to such principles which are made are often no more than dicta. And even where the principles chosen are important to the result attained, that importance is often more apparent than real. For example, if a court chooses to enforce restrictions imposed by a donor in making a gift to a charitable corporation, it can do so on the theory that a charitable trust is involved,[48] or that the corporation holds the gift subject to the condition that it will revert to the donor or his heirs if the restriction is not obeyed,[49] or that the charity contracted with the donor to obey the restriction,[50] or merely because in the particular jurisdiction such restrictions are enforced.[51]

Cases
Involving
Administration

The foregoing cases offer little guidance as to whether corporate principles or trust principles should govern the use to be made by the charitable corporation of the capital gains of its endowment funds. But where the factual situation involves the administration of the charitable corporation, the situation is quite different. (By "administration" we refer to the housekeeping of the corporation, the details of conducting its day-to-day operations and investing its funds.) Corporate principles are applied to the solution of such problems with remarkable uniformity by the courts of all states, regardless of whether they adhere to the trust theory or the theory of absolute ownership for other purposes.[52] And where the courts have not yet mandated the choice of principles to govern such problems, college administrators and text writers seem generally to have assumed that corporate law and not trust law is the applicable standard.

Financial Administration: Where the issue involved is the subject of our particular concern, financial administration, the tendency to apply the principles of corporate law seems especially pronounced.

Asked for his opinion as to the type of investments which can legally be made by an educational institution, the Attorney General of New York stated that the "legal list" which governs investments by trustees has no application to the investment of the endowment funds of the state university. He observed that:

> "Unless modified by statute, charter or by-law, the powers of the trustees of an educational, religious or charitable corporation in respect to the administration and investment of the corporation's funds are fundamentally no different than that of the directors of a business corporation in respect to the administration of the property held by the corporation. . . ."[53]

The Second Restatement of Trusts takes the following flat position:

> "Where money is given to a charitable corporation for its general purposes, it may make such investments as a prudent man would make. Even in a State in which trustees are restricted, by statute or otherwise, to certain kinds of investments, the restriction is not applicable. Even though the corporation is directed to invest the funds and use only the income, either for any of its purposes or for a particular one of its purposes, the restriction applicable to trustees is not applicable to it, unless it is otherwise provided by the terms of the gift."[54]

Trustees are generally forbidden to commingle the funds of separate trusts subject to their care, but substantially all leading educational institutions "pool" their endowment funds. The practice is specifically authorized by statute in a few states, and is now supported by the Second Restatement of Trusts.[55]

Corporate directors have wide discretion to retain earnings as a reserve against future needs; very rarely can stockholders force them to distribute even part of the earnings as dividends.[56] Trustees, on the other hand, in the absence of a specific provision to the contrary in the terms of the trust, must distribute all trust income to the income beneficiary; failure to do so would violate the trustee's duty to administer impartially between the antagonistic interests of the income beneficiary and the remainderman.[57]* It seems to have been assumed everywhere that the

---

*A minor exception to this is the power of trustees to withhold a reasonable amount of income to meet expenses properly chargeable to income.[58]

corporate practice can lawfully be followed by colleges and universities, most if not all of which have retained income at one time or another for "income equalization" reserves or other purposes.

Trustees are under a duty to administer personally the funds subject to their care,[59] while the directors of corporations generally delegate investment duties and retain only general supervisory powers. Here again the directors and trustees of colleges and universities usually follow the practice of their corporate counterparts.[60] The Model Non-Profit Corporation Act permits such delegation to a committee,[61] a practice which the Second Restatement of Trusts also considers to be proper.[62]*

A related problem arises when a charitable corporation transfers all or a substantial part of its assets to another charitable corporation. Such a transfer involves "financial administration" only in a rather broad sense, but the issue involved is one of delegation and for convenience we will discuss the matter here. In Delaware a charitable corporation had transferred over half its endowment to a new charitable foundation. One of the members of the first corporation attacked the transfer, arguing that "an incorporated charitable foundation is governed by the same rules of law as are trustees of a charitable trust," and that the transfer would constitute "a delegation [which] is an abrogation of the trust upon which they hold such funds as trustees."[63] The court held, however, that no technical trust is created by an outright gift to a charitable corporation, but at most a trust in the loose sense of the word, the extent and measure of which are to be determined by the charter and by-laws of the corporation. The court then concluded:

> "This being so, a charitable trust in the technical sense is not created and the test as to the legality of action taken by the governing board of the corporation is to be determined in accordance with principles of corporate law rather than principles governing the fiduciary relationship between trustees of a technical trust and their trust."[64]

The plaintiff pointed to the magnitude of the transfer, but the court said that this was merely a matter of degree, to be left to the judgment of the directors "under familiar principles of corporate law."[65]

An Arkansas court, citing corporate law, upheld a similar transfer on the ground that it had been ratified by the inaction of the members of the transferor charitable corporation, "whose relation to that organi-

---

*Delegation by educational institutions and the few cases in point will be discussed in greater detail later in this report, at pp. 61-65. As we point out there, even if the institution itself were considered a technical trustee subject to the strictures of trust law, its directors should nevertheless be free to delegate investment duties within the corporate structure.

zation is not dissimilar to that of shareholders in the ordinary private corporation."[66]

The words of a Kentucky court, approving a similar transfer as a proper exercise of corporate power, seem particularly apropos:

> "The very nature of the enterprise . . . looked to improvement. It contemplated, by every reasonable implication, that new methods, new people, even new ideas, would be employed, when approved by the governing body of the institution. . . . For the past to bind it to unchangeableness would be to prevent growth, applying the treatment to the head that the Chinese do to the feet."[67]*

Administration in General: As our study widens to include administration generally we find that the courts continue to apply corporate principles as uniformly as they do in regard to matters of financial administration. A typical area relates to the qualification and accountability of the administrator. Even though a testator cloaks his bequest to a charitable corporation in the strictest of trust terminology, the corporation is not required to qualify as a trustee, or post bond, or account to a probate court, as testamentary trustees must do.** For example, the Supreme Judicial Court of Massachusetts was asked in 1955 to construe a bequest to The American Institute of Architects which read in relevant part as follows:

> "[U]pon and subject to the following trusts, uses and conditions: . . . Said principal fund, with all accretions thereto . . . shall be known and designated as 'The Fund'. . . . The capital of the Trust Fund . . . shall be held inviolate for the purposes of the Fund so long as The American Institute of Architects shall endure, and shall not be transferred to any other organization, hypothecated, or distributed in whole or in part until and unless the Institute shall cease to exist. . . ."

The court was asked the following questions:

> "(1) Does the Institute take the gift upon a technical trust subject to appointment and qualification by the Probate Court? or (2) Does the Institute take the gift free of a technical trust but subject to a restriction, being that the gift be used for the particular purposes set forth in the will?"

---

*Most of the courts dealing with the transfer of the assets of one charitable corporation to another appear to have followed the reasoning of the cases quoted in text.[68] Others have treated the matter as one to be determined by an application of the doctrines of cy pres and deviation.[69]

**We refer here to bequests which are intended to be held and administered by the corporation itself for one or more of its own purposes, not to bequests to some third party in trust for the corporation, and not to bequests to the corporation in trust for some third party.

It was held that the latter is the case. The corporation took the bequest not upon a technical trust but rather upon a "quasi-trust" that it follow the testator's restrictions.[70]

Similarly, even where a testator has established a formal trust for charitable purposes and (pursuant to authorization in the will or with permission of a court) the trustee subsequently transfers the trust res to a charitable corporation, the corporation need not thereafter account to the court as a testamentary trustee.[71]

A Pennsylvania statute provides that "pecuniary legacies bequeathed in trust" are to bear interest from the date of the testator's death.[72] Pecuniary bequests which are not in trust bear interest only from the first anniversary of the testator's death. Several charities which had received bequests for their endowment funds argued that the bequests were in trust and that they were therefore entitled to interest from the date of death. They lost. The court said that the legislature was thinking of cases in which income will cease on the death of the life tenant and not be perpetual as in the case of a charity. The latter is not a "trust" in the true sense of the word.[73]*

Similarly, statutory fees for testamentary trustees are irrelevant to bequests to charitable corporations.[74]* A New York statute, for example, regulates commissions for those to whom the Surrogate's Court issues letters of trusteeship.[75] But letters are not issued to educational corporations which simply receive bequests under a will. Logically, since the corporation holds its funds for its own benefit, it would be pointless to compensate itself from those funds.**

Litigation is conducted by the trustee and not the trust, while the charitable corporation itself and not its directors sues or is sued.[76] "[If] a charitable corporation incurs a liability in contract or in tort, an action at law will lie against the corporation, whereas it is only in equity, if at all, that a creditor can reach trust property."[77] Similarly, the charitable corporation itself and not its directors or trustees is a party to the contracts it makes.[78] For example, the New York Court of Appeals held eighty years ago that "trustees of a corporation have no separate or individual authority to bind the corporation, and this although the majority

---

*Note that the issue in these cases could be considered one of financial administration rather than of administration in general, depending upon the scope of one's definition.

**A case in which some institutions deem such compensation worthwhile relates to funds the income of which the donor has restricted to use for specified, limited purposes which may not be high on the institution's list of priorities. A few institutions charge such funds a fee for investment services, and devote the fee to the institution's general purposes.

or the whole number, acting singly and not collectively as a board, should assent to the particular transaction. . . ."[79]

Charitable corporations share with all other corporations the implied power necessary to carry out the express provisions of the corporate charter, such as the power to borrow money and take bequests.[80]*

A charitable corporation also has the power to decide for itself such administrative matters as the qualifications required of its officers and members. Thus a New Jersey court rejected an attack on a local branch of the YWCA, the by-laws of which restricted voting membership to Evangelical Protestants. The restriction was upheld on the ground that all corporations have the power to adopt by-laws to govern matters such as these.[82]

In a recent New York case, the Court of Appeals was asked to decide whether trust principles or corporate principles should govern the removal of the "trustee" of a charitable corporation. A lower court had held that trust principles should apply, because of the similarity between the charitable corporation involved and a charitable trust. In reversing, the Court of Appeals stated the following:

> "The basis of the Appellate Division's determination that this corporation be treated as a trust for the purpose of resolving the legal questions presented was its finding that at the time the Institute was created it was doubtful whether property could be dedicated to charitable purposes through the medium of a trust and that, therefore, the Legislature was asked to create this corporation which was 'sui generis' and 'more nearly resembled a charitable trust than a membership corporation' (25 A D 2d, *supra,* p.290).
>
> "While the Institute disputes the Appellate Division's interpretation of the law of trusts as it existed at the time the Institute was created, it is clear that a corporation and not a trust was created and, regardless of what the law as to trusts was at the time, corporate law and not trust law should govern."[83]

In Pennsylvania a testatrix had directed the formation of a corporation to found and maintain a home for aged gentlewomen. After the home had been in operation for a period of years a resident of the county where it was located brought suit in the Orphans' Court (which has jurisdiction over testamentary trustees) for the removal of the cor-

---

*"A corporation has those powers which are implicit in the charter as well as those which are expressed. Authority not reasonably within the corporate grant is excluded. But whatever may be fairly deemed an incident of the power expressly conferred by the charter is within the grant unless expressly prohibited. The instrument is to receive a reasonable construction to serve the general end in view. . . . There is no distinction in this regard between nonprofit and business corporations."[81]

24

poration's directors, alleging that they had failed to carry out the testatrix's instructions. It was held that that court has no authority to regulate the affairs of any corporation, whether charitable or not.

> "The provision of decedent's will was a bequest to a charitable corporation, not to its directors as trustees for charitable uses. The gift was an outright one, and no trust was created by the will. True, the testatrix used the word 'trustees' in referring to the directors of the corporation, but it is clear from a reading of the will that the term 'trustees' was used simply as a synonym for 'directors,' because she each time referred to them as 'directors or trustees.' Since no trust was established, respondents are not testamentary trustees, and hence not subject for that reason to the jurisdiction of the orphans' court."[84]*

Several cases have involved attempts by charitable corporations to change the locale of their operations (a matter of administration well within the powers of most corporate managements to decide). One such case arose in New Jersey, where suit was brought to restrain a hospital from moving on the theory that the hospital was in reality a charitable trust, and one of the conditions of its founding was that its location not be changed. Despite a long line of New Jersey cases holding in areas not involving administration that trust principles govern charitable corporations, the court refused in this instance to do so, saying:

> "In my opinion defendant is not, strictly speaking, a charitable trust. It is, rather, a charitable corporation, governed by the law applicable to charitable corporations. To some extent this body of doctrine has its roots in the law of trusts, to some extent in the law of corporations; to some extent it may partake of both or indeed be *sui generis*."[87]

The move was held to be within the discretion of the corporation's directors. A Tennessee court rejected an attempt to block the proposed move of a university with the following words:

> "We do not conceive that the general conduct, management, and operation of the corporate entity, nor the handling of its properties generally, can be so controlled [by the cumulative effect of donations from a particular locality], whatever may be the rights reserved to individual contributions in whatever form. One may

---

*Of course the directors of charitable corporations, in common with all other corporate directors, are subject to removal by a court of appropriate jurisdiction if they violate their duty to the corporation or cause it to act outside its corporate powers.[85] Further, charitable corporations and charitable trusts are both subject to the supervision of courts of appropriate jurisdiction at the behest of the attorney general, and in appropriate cases this can entail the removal of the directors or the trustees.[86] But as the quotation set out in text makes clear, this is because charitable corporations and charitable trusts are both charities, not because they both are trusts.

attach such conditions to his contributions as to support his right to withdrawal thereof, upon a violation of such conditions, but his rights, or those of a group so situated, must be so limited. Otherwise it would result that the lawfully constituted directors would be divested of their nondelegable powers, and the corporate control would pass to others who, however great their benefactions, may not thus be lawfully vested with such authority. Fundamental principles of corporate control would thereby be violated."[88]

Finally, consideration should be given to the words of the Chancellor of Delaware, in commenting on recent trends in the judicial construction of legacies to charitable corporations. He noted that many courts:

"lean toward a construction which provides the recipient of such legacies with greater flexibility in their use, if the language permits. . . . Thus, where the doubt as to the proper construction approaches a state of equipoise, I believe the doubt should be resolved against a construction which would require the charitable beneficiary to observe all the requirements applicable to the trustee of an express trust."[89]

Summary of the Existing Law Governing Charitable Corporations

From the foregoing it can readily be seen that the law governing charitable corporations is not merely a branch of trust law, or corporate law, or contract law, but instead is *sui generis,* drawing to some extent on all three of the older disciplines. Where the issue is the ownership of property, courts in all states strain to uphold the claim of the charity involved, rather than see the property lost to private hands. In other cases not involving administration, no general pattern is discernible. But where the issue involves the investment of funds, accounting for their use or other aspects of administration or housekeeping, the courts show a marked tendency to apply corporate principles rather than trust principles, in order to accord charitable corporations a maximum degree of flexibility in their operations. It does not follow that a court faced with the problem must necessarily apply corporate principles in deciding whether realized gain should properly be allocated to principal or to income. It is nevertheless true that the problem is essentially one of administration, and one where the need for flexibility has a particularly strong appeal.

We turn next to a discussion of the law of corporations relating to income.

The Corporate Definition of Income

Statutes which define corporate income or its accumulation, earned surplus, invariably encompass realized appreciation within the scope of their definition. For example, the Model Business Corporation Act defines earned surplus as "the portion of the surplus of a corporation equal to the balance of its net profits, income, gains and losses."[90] Approximately half the jurisdictions in the United States have similar statutes.[91] No statute excludes realized gain from the definition of corporate income. The only controversy in this area has related to the question whether *unrealized* appreciation is included in income, as well as realized gain.*

---

*For example, until the enactment of the Business Corporation Law in 1963, it was held in New York that unrealized appreciation constituted part of earned surplus and was therefore available for the distribution of dividends.[92] The new statute continues to define earned surplus as including "the net earnings, gains or profits, after deduction of all losses," but goes on to provide that "[u]nrealized appreciation of assets is not included in earned surplus."[93] Such an exclusion necessarily leaves *realized* appreciation within the definition. This brings New York into line with other states whose courts have considered the matter.[94]

In the absence of a controlling statutory definition, courts have invariably held that for a corporation, "[p]rofit from the sale of a capital asset—unless the company be in liquidation—enters into earnings or surplus account."[95] In a leading case the New York Court of Appeals was asked to construe the provisions of a corporate charter which provided that holders of the corporation's preferred stock would be entitled to dividends up to a certain amount, if declared, and "to no other or further share of the profits." The corporation had a huge gain or profit on the sale of stocks of other corporations, which it passed through its profit and loss account and proposed to distribute to its common shareholders as a dividend. A large preferred shareholder sued to prevent the distribution, claiming that such gains are in fact accretions to capital, not profits available for dividend distribution. The Court of Appeals unanimously held the gains to be profits (income), not capital (principal), saying:

> "The result of the transaction in question was a profit and the distribution of it is subject to this agreement. This seems so clear that it [is] difficult by discussion to make it more so. The proposition that these profits because resulting from what was perhaps an unusual transaction are not profits, but are an · accretion which 'belongs to capital,' notwithstanding the painstaking argument of counsel, does not seem to have any foundation on which to rest except earnest assertion."[96]

Other Concepts of Income

Professional economists have argued for years over the proper definition of "income", but they do seem to have been virtually unanimous in considering realized gain to be one of its ingredients. The economic concept of income which has now become almost universally accepted by American scholars was first enunciated by Robert M. Haig in 1921.[97] He defined income as "the money value of the net accretion to one's economic power between two points of time" (that is, the increase in one's net worth), plus the money value of goods and services consumed by the individual during the period in question.[98] Henry Simons formulated substantially the same concept in 1938:

> "Personal income may be defined as the alegbraic sum of (1) the market value of rights exercised in consumption and (2) the change in the value of the store of property rights between the beginning and the end of the period in question. . . ."[99]

Note that the Haig-Simons concept would include in income all measurable appreciation, whether or not it is "realized" through sale.[100]*

Realized gains are specifically required to be included in income by the federal income tax law, although under certain circumstances they are taxed at different rates from other types of income.[102] And generally accepted accounting principles require net income to include "all items of profit and loss recognized during the period except for prior period adjustments." This would of course include realized gain. The quotation is from Accounting Principles Board Opinion No. 9, which states that it is meant to have the following application:

> "6. This Opinion applies to general purpose statements which purport to present results of operations in conformity with generally accepted accounting principles. Investment companies, insurance companies and certain nonprofit organizations have developed income statements with formats different from those of the typical commercial entity described herein, designed to highlight the peculiar nature and sources of their income or operating results. The portion of this Opinion *which requires that net income be presented as one amount* does not apply to such entities." (Emphasis supplied.)

Presumably all other portions of the opinion, including the definition of net income, do apply to non-profit corporations.

A proceeding which hinged upon the proper accounting treatment of capital gains involved Alleghany Corporation, the well-known investment company, which was incorporated in 1929 to buy and sell railroad stock. It suffered a large capital loss in 1931 which it deducted directly from paid-in surplus (a capital, or principal, account), as it

---

*It would be more accurate to say that both of them would include in income all realized and unrealized appreciation which represents an increase in the individual's capacity to command goods and services. Both Haig and Simons recognized that appreciation which flows solely from inflation and thus does not increase the individual's actual purchasing power is not income in any real sense.[101] They would therefore adjust putative appreciation by the inflation factor and treat only the excess as income. We shall return to this concept later in this report when we discuss the relevance of the "prudent man" theory to the expenditure of capital gains.

was authorized to do by its charter. It continued in subsequent years to carry all trading gains and losses directly to paid-in surplus. The Securities and Exchange Commission launched an investigation and in 1940 branded the practice improper. Alleghany's charter to the contrary notwithstanding, this was a departure from sound accounting.

> "Accounting authority supports the view that these debits and credits should have been reflected either in the profit and loss statements or carried directly to earned surplus, preferably the former.
> ". . . .
> "Carrying the losses directly to paid-in surplus had the net effect of understating that account and overstating the earned surplus account in the financial statements of Alleghany filed with us. Thus, accumulated earnings were apparently left intact. According to present day accounting principles, this would be improper."[103]

In point of fact the only body of learning which treats realized gains as anything other than income is the law of trusts, which was developed to accommodate the divergent interests of income beneficiaries and remaindermen. And even in the trust area traditional views of principal and income are being brought into question. Professor Allison Dunham, Executive Director of the National Conference of Commissioners on Uniform State Laws and the principal draftsman of the Revised Uniform Principal and Income Act, called recently for a reexamination of the whole subject in a speech which ended with the following words:

> "If the life of the law is experience, as Mr. Justice Holmes wrote, we should begin applying 20th Century experience rather than the logical assumptions of the 19th Century investment experience."[104]

The changes to which Professor Dunham alludes are primarily those which have taken place in the field of investments.

Financial and Investment Trends

For at least the past three decades the investment community in general has been concentrating with ever-increasing emphasis on the long-term growth potential of investments and paying proportionately less attention to the current return of dividends and interest.[105] In part this may be due to a recognition that for the past century the annual return* on unselected common stocks as a group has been double that of high-quality fixed income securities.[106] An important factor has certainly been the desire of investors to provide some safeguard against inflation's continuing erosion of the purchasing power of the dollar.[107] These points are so well recognized that they do not warrant elaboration here.

Another factor has been the two-fold impact of income tax laws on corporations and investors. With tax brackets as they are, it would be unthinkable for a corporation to distribute all its earnings as dividends and then go back to its stockholders and offer them stock to obtain funds for expansion. Many corporations therefore have adopted the practice of retaining 50% or more of their annual earnings. In some extreme cases they pay out nothing.** As retained earnings accumulate and multiply, they are commuted into appreciation (higher market value of the corporation's shares) that can be realized upon sale.[108] This alternative is attractive to the typical investor, who must pay full taxes on dividends and interest but only 25% or less on realized appreciation.***

For a number of reasons, then, our economy has come to value realized appreciation and to find means to commute or divert earnings

---

*Including gains as well as dividends.

**The elimination of dividends for the purpose of stimulating the growth of capital gains is strongly advocated by Carol J. Loomis in an article in the June 15, 1968 issue of *Fortune* entitled "A Case for Dropping Dividends." She observes (at p. 181):

> "In a period when corporate capital is scarce, when corporate investment opportunities are expanding, and when capital gains are taxed at low rates, it's clearer than ever that dividends are a 'bad buy' for most stockholders."

She goes on to state (*ibid.*):

> "Under today's tax laws, any taxpaying stockholder who gets his returns through dividends rather than capital gains is odds on to come out second-best."

***This alternative is attractive for the additional reason that a taxpaying investor to a large extent has freedom of choice as to the taxable year in which he realizes appreciation.

from dividends to appreciation. Many of these reasons are inapplicable to charitable corporations because they are tax-exempt, but since they are not the only investors they must fit within the present system.

In some respects charitable corporations are in a unique position to derive even more benefit from the growing emphasis on appreciation than most other investors can derive.* Nevertheless, if educational institutions are forbidden to utilize as income any of the earnings which our society has commuted into appreciation, many of them will continue to favor high yield-low growth investments to the detriment of future generations.[110]

Proper Classification
of Realized Appreciation

At this point it may be helpful to summarize briefly the highlights of our report thus far, insofar as they relate to the classification of realized gains of endowment funds as principal or income:

(1) Our survey of typical donative instruments indicates that donors of endowment funds have in the past almost never specified whether realized gains must be retained as principal or may be expended as income.

(2) Statutes leave the question open in virtually all the states, and the courts have not yet spoken.

(3) Corporate law and trust law both offer solutions, but they are diametrically opposed.

---

*Being tax-exempt they attain flexibility which is denied to taxpayers. Artificial barriers such as the six-month long-term capital gains holding period become meaningless. When a sale is made the institution can enjoy the full benefit of any realization which does occur. They can realize gains whenever the need arises, without suffering the tax consequences which plague other investors. Because they need not liquidate their investments in the manner of a bank or insurance company, the risks of a sharp but temporary fall in market values are less serious for them.[109]

(4) In determining what principles to apply to the solution of the problem, the question is not whether a charitable corporation is the "absolute owner" of its property or merely holds it "in trust." No jurisdiction treats charitable corporations exactly like business corporations or exactly like trusts for all purposes; all jurisdictions apply the principles of corporate law to the solution of some of their problems, and the principles of trust law to the solution of others. The choice of principles depends upon the factual situation before the court.

(5) Where the issue involved is not one of administration, the only clearly discernible judicial trend or attitude is a marked tendency to favor charities in their disputes with others over property, and corporate law or trust law is used less for guidance than to rationalize the desired result.

(6) Where the issue involved is one of administration, particularly financial administration, courts uniformly tend to apply the more flexible principles found in corporate law.

(7) To an ever-increasing extent dividends are being commuted by our investment community into capital gains. They are treated as interchangeable by economists, accountants, tax lawyers and corporate lawyers. Only under trust law are they considered basically different.

We are thus led to the conclusion that there is no substantial authority under existing law to support the widely held view that the realized gains of endowment funds of educational institutions must be treated as principal. No case has been found which holds that such an institution does not have the legal right to determine for itself whether to retain all such gains or to expend a prudent part. We submit that there is no reason why the law should deny educational institutions that flexibility.

There are those who argue that if the law does not in fact bar the spending of capital gains, the "sluice gates" will open wide and all our educational endowment will drain away. Such an argument is necessarily premised on the assumption that our colleges and universities are directed by irresponsible men who await only the opportunity to dissipate the funds committed to their care. We believe that assumption is ill-founded. But if fear does exist that expenditures might in individual cases exceed the bounds of prudence, the courts could and should define those bounds in a logical adaptation of the traditional Prudent Man Rule. We discuss this at greater length below.*

---

*See pp. 40-47, *infra*.

If colleges and universities are in fact legally free to treat capital gains as expendable income, several questions immediately present themselves. Must such treatment be limited to realized appreciation, or does it logically apply to unrealized appreciation as well? *Must* all realized gains be expended as they are earned? If realized gains are retained beyond the year in which they are earned, may they be spent in later years? If capital gains are spent, how can the purchasing power of principal be maintained in periods of inflation? How should capital losses be handled? These questions will be considered seriatim.

Is Unrealized Appreciation Income? To most economists the "realization" of gains and losses is an artificial, almost meaningless concept. Assume that an educational institution holds two securities, each of which is now worth $100. Security "A" originally cost $150, while security "B" cost $50. In terms of economic power the institution is exactly where it was when it purchased the two; it still holds securities worth an aggregate of $200. If it sells either security and retains the other, it will have $100 in cash and a security worth $100. But depending upon which security it chooses to sell, it will be said to have "realized" a gain or a loss of $50—even if it immediately repurchases the security it sold. Economists emphasize that in reality the institution is neither better nor worse off for having gone through the exercise of selling and buying back, and the logic of their position seems unassailable.

Such reasoning seems especially cogent when applied to educational institutions. Being tax-exempt, a college or university is free at any time to sell its entire portfolio of marketable securities or any portion of it, and to buy it back immediately, at no greater cost than the brokerage fees and transfer taxes involved. Except for that cost, such a transaction would not change its economic position in the slightest. It is not the sale and buy-back which increase or decrease its purchasing power, but the gradual appreciation or diminution of the market value of its portfolio which preceded those transactions. For this reason a growing number of people disregard realization and look instead to changes in market value to measure income or loss.[111]

But in this report we are discussing the law as it exists and as it is likely to find expression in the judicial opinions of the foreseeable future. It is enough to ask the courts to take one major step within the bounds of traditional thinking. To depart from the concept of realization would be to cast tradition completely aside. The courts have always considered realization to be an essential ingredient of income, whether they were

34

defining corporate profits[112] or trust income.[113]* Our income tax laws reflect this thinking,[116] although proposals for a change are from time to time advanced.[117] In light of this we consider it to be quite unlikely that a court today would regard the unrealized appreciation of an endowment fund as expendable income, and we have therefore limited our discussion to the proper classification of realized gains alone.

Must All Gains be Spent as Earned?   One of the indispensable tools of successful financial management is flexibility, and for colleges and universities flexibility necessarily connotes the freedom to save fully as much as it connotes the freedom to spend. At times it may be imperative that an educational institution be able to husband its funds. In practice virtually all educational institutions at one time or another have retained income from their endowment funds beyond the year in which it was earned. The Department of Health, Education and Welfare found in a 1963 survey that over half of the reporting educational institutions with endowment over $5 million have permanent reserves to protect principal, and 40% have income stabilization reserves.[118] The American Council on Education has recommended that both types of reserves be maintained.[119] And if the expenses of an endowed professorship, for example, are less in a given year than the income of that endowment, it seems to be the universal practice to retain the excess income for use in a future year for the purpose specified. Indeed it is difficult to see what else the institutions could do with such an excess, since they would be subject to attack if they diverted it to some use other than the one specified by the donors.[120]

If dividends and interest can be thus retained, it seems clear that colleges and universities should have at least the same power to retain capital gains if they choose to do so, regardless of the classification of capital gains as income. The question thus presented is whether the law sanctions the prevailing practice of educational institutions. To answer that question we turn first to the typical donative instruments which were discussed earlier in this report,** to determine the extent to which they give the donee institutions discretion over the expenditure or retention of income.

As was mentioned earlier, instruments covering about 5% of the

---

*As we noted above, an exception to this in respect of business corporations could be found in New York prior to 1963. It had there been held that unrealized appreciation constituted part of earned surplus and was therefore available for the distribution of dividends.[114] This was changed by the new Business Corporation Law, and appreciation must now be realized before it can be taken into account in computing earnings.[115]

**See pp. 9-12, *supra*.

aggregate value of the funds studied employed formal trust language in describing the grant, and because of uncertainty as to the extent to which this circumstance might lead a court to require the use of trust principles in the administration of the grant, such instruments have been excluded from the scope of this memorandum.

Only four of the 462 instruments studied, covering about 1½% of the aggregate value of the funds involved, by their terms require the expenditure of all income annually or as it is received. Another ten instruments, covering less than 2% of the aggregate value of the funds involved, require that income be "spent," but without reference to a time period; the terms of these instruments would appear to be met if income were set aside in whole or in part for expenditure in a future year or years for the designated purpose.

A far larger number of instruments, covering 27% of the aggregate value of the funds involved, require that income be "used" or "applied" for designated purposes. Presumably the allocation of a portion of income to an income-producing reserve fund would satisfy the terms of such instruments as well as would immediate expenditure, provided that the earnings of such fund be dedicated solely to the designated purpose.

Another group, covering about 19% of the aggregate value of the funds studied, give the institution or its officers full discretion as to the use to which income is to be put. Such discretion would clearly include the right to allocate a portion of income to principal or to an income-producing reserve fund.

Some instruments, covering 5% of the aggregate value of the funds studied, specifically give the donee institutions discretion to accumulate or spend income. A smaller number, covering 2% of the value of the funds studied, direct that any income not used is to be added to principal. And a very few instruments, covering a fraction of one per cent of the aggregate value of the funds involved, require the accumulation of all income for a designated period, or the addition to principal of a percentage of each year's income.

The largest group of instruments, covering 38% of the value of the funds studied, do not even refer to income as such. Nothing in their terms would restrict the free exercise of discretion by the donee institutions over the expenditure or accumulation of income.

In summary, then, instruments covering only 1½% of the aggregate value of the funds studied would appear to require expenditure of all income (presumably including capital gains, if they were considered to be income) in the year in which it is earned. All of the remaining instruments which were considered relevant for this purpose (covering 93% of the aggregate value of the funds studied) would by their terms permit (and in some cases would direct) the donee institution to retain income for expenditure in the future or to add it to principal.

Turning to the law, we find in this area as in so many others a dearth of direct authority as to the principles which are to be applied to charitable corporations. The fact that the practice of accumulating portions of endowment income from time to time is so widespread may itself constitute the strongest evidence that the practice is legally permissible. In this respect accumulation may be akin to the pooling of endowment funds, which gained almost universal acceptability without statutory or judicial authority.* The wisdom of pooling came to be recognized because of the economies it offered by doing away with piecemeal management. The reasonable accumulation of reserves for the protection of principal and future income has an even longer history in the practice of charitable corporations, and an even stronger basis for support in reason.

If the principles which govern business corporations are applicable to accumulations by charitable corporations, as the administrators of endowment funds seem generally to have assumed, reasonable accumulations can be said to have the full sanction of the law. As we indicated earlier, the directors of business corporations have wide discretion in the husbanding of the corporation's funds to meet its future needs.[123]

Even if trust principles are applied, however, it is unlikely that reasonable accumulations by charitable corporations would be struck down by the courts. A trustee for a private trust is under a duty to avoid favoring either the income beneficiary or the remainderman at the expense of the other, and for that reason he cannot withhold income from the income beneficiary but must pay it over at reasonable intervals (for example, quarterly) as it is earned.[124]** But in the case of charitable corporations there are not two antagonistic beneficiaries but only one, the corporation itself, and so the reason for the rule vanishes.[126]

More directly in point is the statutory or common law rule which prohibits fiduciaries from accumulating income beyond a limited number of years or beyond a "reasonable" period, regardless of directions to

---

*As we have indicated earlier in this report, pooling has now been specifically authorized by statutes in several states[121] and has received the prestigious support of the Restatement (Second) of Trusts.[122] These are reflections of the practice rather than well-springs of it. It had no such basis of authority when it became widespread three decades ago.

**Even this is subject to some exceptions. For example, the trustee can properly build up income reserves to meet anticipated expenses which will properly be charged to income.[125]

the contrary in the donative instrument. This rule is bottomed not on a desire to protect the interests of the income beneficiary, but on the interest of society in avoiding undue concentrations of economic power and the withholding of property for too long a period from those it was intended to benefit.[127] The rule applies only to property held in a fiduciary capacity; a person is free to accumulate his own income, if he chooses to do so.[128] There is some doubt about whether the common law rule and at least some of the statutes apply to charitable corporations; applicability depends upon whether the corporation is deemed to hold its property in "trust," and we have already seen that such an inquiry can be an unrewarding exercise in semantics.[129]

The common law rule is in force in most states, since only a minority have enacted statutes dealing with accumulations. As applied to charities the common law rule merely subjects accumulations to judicial supervision, with the guidelines that accumulations are to be upheld if they are reasonable in time and amount in light of all the circumstances.[130] The courts have been lenient, upholding a variety of accumulations for indefinite or quite lengthy periods.[131] And where the retention of income is "found to be merely in the course of judicious management of the trust," it does not even constitute an accumulation subject to the rule.[132] The retention of capital gains by a charitable corporation, at least to the extent necessary to compensate for inflation, would seem to be a clear example of "judicious management."* This is uniquely true in the case of educational institutions, virtually all of which are in urgent need of current revenue; a retention of income by such institutions can safely be assumed to reflect a prudent concern for the needs of the future, and not an ambition to accumulate wealth for its own sake.

In those jurisdictions which have enacted statutes some have exempted charities from their application, in whole or in part.[135] None of the others pose any real problem for educational institutions, for the reasons discussed above in connection with the common law rule.[136]**

---

*The Restatement of Property, from which the quotation in text was taken, failed to take a position on whether the retention of income to preserve trust assets against a decline in purchasing power would constitute an accumulation subject to the rule. The reporters felt that the absence of decisions in point made an attempt to restate the law in that regard premature.[133] But even if such a retention is considered an accumulation, it seems quite clear that it is one which the courts should consider reasonable, and thus permissible under the rule.[134]

**Note, however, a California statute which provides that:
"Except as specially approved by the Attorney General [a charitable] corporation shall not accumulate income for a period longer than five years."[137]
Even if the retention of capital gains were considered to be an accumulation of income subject to the statute, it seems unlikely that the Attorney General would withhold his consent, particularly if the retention were for the purpose of preserving the purchasing power of an endowment in an inflationary period.

38

In an analogous field, the Treasury Department has ruled that the retention by a charitable corporation of capital gains from the sale of investment property, when the gains are reinvested within a reasonable time in similar property, will not constitute an accumulation which would deprive the corporation of its exemption from income taxes.[138]*

In summary, then, it would appear that educational institutions would continue to be free to preserve all or part of the realized appreciation of their endowment funds if they chose to do so, regardless of the classification of such appreciation as income. There is nothing in the law as it now exists which would condemn such a retention, it would not violate the terms of typical donative instruments, and it would accord with the time-honored practice of educational institutions in their handling of dividends and interest.

May Gains Which Are Retained be Spent in Future Years? Several writers, in articles emphasizing the inviolability of the principal of endowment, have suggested that funds available for current use which have nevertheless been voluntarily placed in endowment by the institution which receives them can never thereafter be removed.[140] If this were an accurate statement of the law it could pose at least a theoretical problem for those institutions which have allowed gains to accumulate in endowment over the years. It could be argued that even though the institutions were legally free to spend such gains as they were realized, they chose not to do so but instead committed them to endowment, where they must now remain.**

Such an argument seems an exercise in sophistry. Accumulation of gains in endowment cannot realistically be said to be a conscious commitment by an institution which is unaware of its right to spend them. And even if it were, it would be unreasonable for the law to use the choice of one generation of directors in an internal matter such as this to tie the hands of all future directors, through all eternity. But be that as it may, the suggestion of the writers is simply not an accurate statement of the law. None of them cited any judicial authority in support of their theory, and with the exception of a dictum by a lower court in New York we have been unable to find any.[141]*** The only cases found

---

*Colleges and universities are not subject in any event to the provision which deprives charitable corporations of their exemptions for unreasonable accumulations.[139]

**A similar problem is posed by misclassification. It will be recalled that in our survey of typical donative instruments we found that 22% of the instruments classified by the institutions as endowment contained no legal prohibition whatsoever against spending principal, and a number specifically permitted it.

***Of course if an institution solicits gifts upon the representation that they will be placed in

which were directly in point held to the contrary. In Massachusetts a charitable corporation had established a charity fund, the income only of which could be expended, under the direction of certain "trustees." Fifty-six years later the corporation was permitted to transfer the money in the charity fund to its general fund, on the ground that it could deal with its assets as it saw fit, despite the earlier classification.[144] And in a well-known Nebraska decision the court protected the endowment funds of an insolvent college from the claims of creditors by construing them as charitable trusts. Such protection only extended to funds placed in endowment at the direction of the donor, however. Other funds which the institution had voluntarily classified as endowment, although with the consent of the donor, were considered to be the institution's own property, reachable by its creditors.[145]

Even the writers who would prevent reclassification of funds would do so only in the case of funds allocated to endowment. If they were labelled "Funds for Special Purposes" or "Funds Functioning as Endowment," the writers are in agreement that they can be expended in whole or in part at any time in the discretion of the institution.[146] Although such a distinction seems a pointless emphasis of form over substance, it would of course be preferable from the point of view of the institution to avoid argument and possible attack by adopting a special label for realized gains it wishes to retain.

Application of the Prudent Man Rule: As we indicated above, a broader interpretation of income is more likely to find ready acceptance if reasonable guidelines are developed to govern its expenditure. The standard by which directors of a charitable corporation are most often judged in the administration of the corporation's affairs is that which "a man of common prudence ordinarily exercises in his own affairs."[147]* Even if a charitable corporation otherwise has total freedom under the law to spend all of the gains of its endowment funds as they are realized, as well as interest and dividends, it may well be questioned whether it would be prudent to do so.

Later in this report we discuss the quality of prudence demanded of fiduciaries in the investment of funds.** But the standards developed

---

endowment, the representation is enforced.[142] And where early records were missing and the institution could not tell whether restrictions had been imposed by donors or had voluntarily been assumed by the institution itself, the court refused to resolve the doubt by striking down the restrictions.[143] But such cases are readily distinguishable from the situation discussed in text.

*Substantially the same yardstick has been used to measure the conduct of directors of business corporations[148] and of trustees.[149]

***See pp. 56-61, *infra*.

in that connection offer little help in defining guidelines of permissible conduct in the expenditure of capital gains. The problem is new to the law, and because it is different from past problems the solution will be different from past solutions. But whatever nuances may be embodied in its final form, the solution is likely to be grounded upon the requirement of prudence, which the dictionary defines as "practical wisdom," or the "provident or cautious use of resources."[150]

The profound changes in financial and investment trends over the past several decades, discussed earlier in this report,* have led a number of people to conclude that the traditional discipline of spending currently no more than the dividends and interest earned by capital is not the only way of exercising prudence. Thus institutions such as the Museum of Modern Art now appropriate each year a fixed percentage (usually based on the average yield on prime bonds over the long term) of the average market value of their funds over the past several years, without regard to dividends and interest received. Yale does substantially the same, but it fixes the return expected from its funds each year by analyzing and balancing its needs and resources to arrive at what it terms the "University Equation."[151] A similar practice is now followed by Cornell and the University of Chicago with respect to their unrestricted or "quasi-endowment funds" (that is, funds the principal of which may legally be spent, but which the institution has decided to retain for investment).[152] Cornell's treasurer explained the creation of its unrestricted "Capital Fund" as follows:

> "This Capital Fund has been created for the express purpose of freeing ourselves from the restraining influence of the income factor. We want to buy securities simply to make money, and in this Fund we have no concern whether the product be labeled income or capital gain. We can use either. This does not mean that we are abandoning the fundamental principal of prudence and that we are embarking on a speculative spree; it does mean that some new risks will be taken, and that to the interested observer, our posture is likely to appear more aggressive than heretofore."[153]

Other formulae include one adopted by the American Economic Association, which includes in income not only dividends and interest received but a proportionate share of the earnings retained by the companies whose securities are held by the Association, and takes account as well of fluctuations in the market value of the securities over the past three years.[154]

---

*See pp. 31-32, *supra.*

One of the basic principles underlying both the traditional discipline and the new formulae is that some reasonable control is needed to prevent the irresponsible dissipation of funds. Proponents of the new formulae argue that they are fully as effective in this respect as the traditional discipline while more accurately reflecting present-day realities, and that in addition they free investment managers to select securities without undue emphasis on their current yield.

We believe that the courts will eventually hold that the realized appreciation of endowment funds constitutes income. They may also hold that such appreciation can be spent to the full extent called for by such formulae, but it seems to us more likely that certain safeguards will be imposed to govern the expenditure of realized gains. If this is so institutions will of course be free to adopt any prudent formula they wish to adopt to provide guidelines for an appropriate return from their investment funds, and unrestricted funds can be appropriated in whole or in part to provide that return. The safeguards of which we speak, if indeed they are imposed by the courts, will merely bear on the extent to which the realized gains of true endowment funds can be drawn upon to meet the return called for by the institution's formula.

One of the safeguards most likely to commend itself to the courts relates to inflation. As we stressed at the outset of our report, a basic criticism of the investment policies of many college and university endowment funds is that they fail to foster the growth of their capital sufficiently to compensate for the incessant erosion of inflation. If the policies are changed to foster growth but all gains are spent as they are realized, without taking inflation into account, it seems clear that there may be no long-term benefit to the institution.

As was pointed out earlier, economists such as Haig and Simons define income basically as an increase in purchasing power.* As every housewife knows, appreciation which does no more than keep pace with the rising cost of living is not an increase in any real sense. In time of inflation, paychecks cannot buy more groceries unless they include "raises" in salary which exceed the rise in the cost of living.

The prudent man concerned with the safety of his capital would retain enough of his realized gains to compensate for losses due to inflation, and it seems logical to assume that most administrators of college and university endowment funds would deem it prudent to do the same. We believe that this would be the starting point of most courts in

---

*See pp. 28-29, *supra*.

formulating guidelines for prudent conduct in this area.

Another area of concern relates to realized losses. Despite the general trend of the stock market for the past three decades it is nevertheless true that what goes up is capable of coming down, and it would be a truly unique investment manager who never made a single wrong guess. For this reason it would seem imprudent to spend all realized gains in one year without making some provision for losses which may be realized the next. A ready answer is suggested by the income stabilization reserves which many colleges and universities have maintained for years. Some of the dividends and interest which are earned in relatively prosperous years are husbanded in a reserve which is drawn upon in lean years, thus smoothing over the peaks and valleys of investment revenue. The same thing could easily be done with respect to realized gains and losses.* Presumably the reserve would be somewhat larger in proportion to the gains involved than dividend-and-interest reserves have been in the past, because of the greater irregularity with which gains are realized. The proportion of gains assigned to such a reserve would also presumably vary in inverse proportion to the appreciation in market value of the institution's endowment; as the market value of an endowment rises higher above its book value, the danger posed by the possible realization of a loss in an individual security diminishes, and so does the need for a reserve to guard against such a loss. Further, the volatility of the endowment's investments has a bearing on the size of the reserve required; the risk of loss as well as the prospect of gain is greater in the case of a portfolio which is subject to wide swings in market value.

Parenthetically, it should be noted that most colleges and universities have some margin of safety in respect of investment losses, in that the current market value of their endowment funds exceeds the original or book value. As we stated earlier, for purposes of this report we polled all institutions of higher learning in the United States with investment portfolios having a market value of $3,000,000 or more as of June 30, 1967. Of the responding institutions, 148 furnished both the original and market values of their endowment. The aggregate endowment of the responding institutions had an original value (unadjusted for subsequent fluctuations, whether realized or unrealized) of $1,786,000,000 and a market value of $3,023,000,000, or an average appreciation of 69%.

---

*Realized gains and losses are already carried in a separate account by most educational institutions, according to a 1963 survey of endowment funds conducted by the Department of Health, Education and Welfare. As has been mentioned, the same survey found that more than half of the responding institutions with endowments of $5 million or more maintained reserves for the protection of principal, and 40% maintained income stabilization reserves.[155]

Examined individually, the returns presented a less favorable picture. One institution reported a market value less than the original value, several reported no appreciation, and only half reported appreciation of 30% or more.*

To return to the Prudent Man Rule and its application to the expenditure of realized appreciation, it may be helpful for us to present a few illustrations of how the general theories we have suggested might be applied in practice. Assume for this purpose that a college has an endowment which in 1948 contained securities valued at $1,000,000 in terms of both original value and market value.** By 1968 the market value of the securities in the endowment has grown to $1,450,000, but after referring to various price indices the college's board of directors determines that $1,400,000 of that market value represents the original purchasing power of the endowment. Only the remaining $50,000 of the increment represents true appreciation.***

(1) Assume that the college realized $40,000 in gains from the sale of securities during 1968, but also realized $40,000 in losses from such sales. Would it be prudent to spend part of the realized gains? We believe not. The institution has neither profited nor lost by sales of securities during the year; its net gain from that source is zero. It would

---

*The funds described in text are "pure endowment funds"; that is, funds the principal of which must be maintained intact and in perpetuity. The institutions were also asked about investment funds the principal of which they are free to spend, if they choose to do so. These are sometimes called "quasi-endowment funds" or "funds functioning as endowment." Such funds of the responding institutions have an aggregate original value of $772,000,000 and a current market value of $1,200,000,000, or an average appreciation of 55%. Seventeen of the institutions had no such funds. Of those which did, half reported either no appreciation or appreciation of less than 30% of original value.

**The year 1948 has been chosen for purposes of illustration because the great bulk of the appreciation of endowment funds has come into being since that year. Prior to that time the managers of most endowment funds (and most other institutional investors) kept the bulk of their assets in bonds and other fixed-income investments which did not allow capital to grow. The gradual increase since that date in the ratio of equity to debt in the holdings of endowment funds has coincided with (and to a large extent has been directly attributable to) a comparatively steady rise in the market values of equity securities.[156] It should also be noted that the inroads of inflation in the United States, while not entirely a post-war phenomenon, have nevertheless been more pronounced during this period than in any comparable period in our history.[157]

For simplicity we have ignored contributions to our hypothetical endowment since 1948. In practice yearly adjustments for inflation (or deflation) would be made for such contributions also, treating each year's contributions as a separate fund for this purpose. The aggregate book values of each year's contributions, added to that of the endowment as it existed in the chosen base year (in our hypothetical, 1948), in each case adjusted upward to account for inflation, would constitute the current book value for the entire endowment fund, as so adjusted.

***The appreciation of our hypothetical endowment is less than the average appreciation of 69% reported by the institutions which responded to our questionnaire, but somewhat more than the median appreciation of 30%.

We have limited our discussion to the treatment of gains and losses realized from the sale of marketable securities. A discussion of specialized problems relating to other types of investments, such as the appropriate treatment of depreciation of real property, would unduly lengthen the report.

44

clearly be unrealistic to take only gains into account and ignore all losses. This conclusion is not changed by the fact that the institution has unrealized appreciation in addition to its realized gains. While it is true that if the institution had liquidated its portfolio it would have had a net expendable gain of $50,000, in fact it chose not to do so. For the reasons explained earlier we do not believe that the courts would classify unrealized appreciation as expendable income. For this reason we feel constrained to maintain the distinction and draw the line between realized and unrealized gains.

(2) Assume that the college realizes $50,000 in net gains from the sale of securities during 1968. Would it be prudent to spend the entire amount? We believe not; it would be wiser to hold some portion as a reserve against possible losses in the future, particularly in view of the fact that the market value of the endowment is relatively close to its original value as adjusted for inflation.

(3) Assume that the college has a reserve for gains and losses from the sale of securities, but losses realized in 1967 left the reserve with a negative balance of $30,000. In 1968 the college realizes net gains of $100,000 from the sale of securities. How much of this could prudently be spent? We believe that a prudent man dealing with his own funds who wishes to preserve their purchasing power would retain a portion of the gain sufficient to eliminate the negative balance in the reserve and establish some positive balance to guard against possible future losses. Even if the college had started the year with a positive balance in the reserve it would be imprudent to spend more than $50,000 of the gains, because to do so would diminish the purchasing power of the endowment below its original level (as adjusted for subsequent inflation).

(4) Assume that the college realizes a net loss of $60,000 from the sale of securities, and that the balance in its reserve for gains and losses from the sale of securities is only $30,000. Must it retain $30,000 of income from dividends and interest to make up the deficit? We believe not, even if the market value of the endowment falls below the book value as adjusted for inflation. There is no authority under existing law and practice for the imposition of such a requirement, and we submit that it would be unwise and undesirable to include such a requirement in the guidelines of prudent conduct which will be promulgated by the courts if capital gains of endowment funds are permitted to be expended as income.

To an extent this could be said to be inconsistent with our basic position, that realized gains may properly be treated as income. If gains and losses must be balanced against each other to arrive at net income from sales of securities, it could logically be argued that the net gain or loss from such sales must be added to or subtracted from income from dividends and interest to arrive at an overall net income from endowment.

But neither charitable corporations nor trusts are required under existing law or practice to retain dividends or interest if they suffer a loss on the sale of investment securities. They are not required to accumulate income if the market value of their endowment funds falls below the book value as adjusted for inflation, and in the absence of instructions in the donative instrument they are not even required to accumulate income if the market value falls below the unadjusted book value. Business corporations are forbidden to distribute dividends to their stockholders when capital is impaired, but the purpose of that rule is to protect creditors of the corporation.[158] The same considerations do not apply to an impairment of the principal of the endowment funds of charitable corporations, and therefore no similar restriction has heretofore been imposed upon them.

Does the treatment of capital gains as income require the development of guidelines stricter than those which the law has imposed in the past? To an extent we have felt that it does, in recognition of the fact that the expenditure of capital gains would constitute a new, more liberal practice for most educational institutions. The concept of adjusting the book value of endowment funds to compensate for inflation is a step beyond the existing requirements of the law which we feel would commend itself to the courts and to most prudent administrators. It would meet the justifiable concern that the purchasing power of the funds might be seriously impaired. For the same reason we have suggested that some portion of realized gains be retained as a reserve against possible future losses. But it does not follow that dividends and interest must also be matched against such losses. The imposition of such a requirement would not only go beyond existing law but would deprive educational institutions of the flexibility the courts have striven to give them, and would do so at a time when the need for such flexibility is most vital. The development of guidelines of prudence in this general area is an exercise in reason and common sense, and by that test this restriction would go too far.

In summary, we believe that the guidelines of prudent conduct relating to the expenditure by charitable corporations of realized gains of their endowment funds should appropriately provide for the retention of a sufficient portion of gains to maintain the purchasing power of the funds in periods of inflation, and should also provide for the establishment of a reserve against the possible realization of future losses. We do not believe that prudence would dictate the retention of dividends and interest to balance such losses.

Means of Classifying
Realized Gains
as Income

We have concluded that it would be desirable for educational institutions to have the flexibility in their investment planning which would flow from classifying realized gains as income. We have also concluded that there is nothing in the terms of typical donative instruments or in the law as it now exists which would stand in the way of such classification. It is nevertheless true that it has been the traditional practice of most cautious administrators of educational endowment funds to classify realized gains as principal. To bring about a change in this practice will require some sort of affirmative action. Various alternatives in this regard are discussed below.

Declaratory Judgment: The most expeditious method of resolving doubts about the legality of classifying realized gains of endowment funds as income would be to ask the courts for a declaratory judgment. We believe that it would be in the best interests of higher education for one or more such suits to be brought in the near future. It is conceivable that the courts will hold against the petitioning institutions, but this would hardly leave them in a worse position than the one they now occupy. Until the courts have spoken, few lawyers will feel able to advise colleges and universities that they are perfectly safe in departing from the traditional practice of retaining all realized gains of endowment funds. A favorable decision of the courts would open the way for such advice, and for all the reasons set forth above we believe the decision should be favorable.

The suits should be brought by institutions which have successfully invested their endowment in growth stocks, and feel restrained by the uncertainty of the law from spending even a fraction of the gains which they have realized. Our study indicates that New York is the jurisdiction where the trend of judicial decisions makes a favorable result most likely. The concentration of charitable institutions in New York and its role in finance combine to create a climate sympathetic to changing needs. Further, the New York Court of Appeals decided the historic case of *St. Joseph's Hosp. v. Bennett,* 281 N.Y. 115, 22 N.E.2d 305 (1939), which itself was initiated by an action seeking a declaratory judgment.

Legislation and its Problems: Another means to the same end would be legislation. Unlike a judicial decision, which often influences courts outside the jurisdiction where it is pronounced, a statute is effective only within the boundaries of the particular state which promulgates it. This would require deliberations by the legislatures of all 50 states, if the entire country were to benefit.

But the legislative approach could have one advantage which we believe cannot now be derived from a declaratory judgment. Legislation could eliminate the requirement that gains and losses must be "realized" before they are taken into account in defining income. We have indicated earlier in this report that the concept of realization is an artificial and cumbersome ingredient in the definition of income.* An institution can realize a gain in an individual security when its overall endowment is worth less than its original value, and it can realize a loss even though the value of the endowment as a whole has multiplied many times. The important point of reference is the overall appreciation or depreciation of the endowment, not the realization of splintered fractions which bear no necessary correlation to the whole. This can be taken into account in determining whether it is prudent to expend realized gains, as we have suggested.** A more satisfactory approach would be to disregard realization in the statutory definition of the principal of an endowment which must be maintained intact. Such a definition would start with the original dollar value of the fund, would provide for its adjustment upward or downward to reflect changes in the purchasing power of the

---

*See pp. 34-35, *supra.*

**See pp. 40-47, *supra.*

dollar since the fund was received by the institution, and might provide for the retention of a percentage of the adjusted total to serve as a buffer against a possible future decline in the purchasing power of the fund. Appreciation in excess of that amount could be expended as income in the discretion of the institution.

It is beyond the scope of this report to suggest the specific wording of a model act to govern the administration of the endowment funds of institutions of higher education. Ideally such an act would establish standards:

(1) for the selection of suitable investments, preferably giving due recognition to the fact that today's Prudent Man is concerned not only with the safety of the original dollar value of his principal, but also with the preservation of its purchasing power;

(2) for the utilization of income, preferably by defining endowment, principal and income in light of the Prudent Man Rule along the lines suggested in this report; and

(3) for miscellaneous matters of administration such as the delegation of investment responsibilities and the pooling of funds for purposes of investment.

The National Conference of Commissioners on Uniform State Laws and the American Law Institute are both charged with the responsibility of preparing such model acts, and are particularly well suited for the task. We earnestly commend this subject to their attention.

As previously noted, in January 1969 New York's Joint Legislative Committee to Study Revision of Corporation Laws submitted to the legislature a bill which would apply to not-for-profit corporations generally (but not to most educational institutions, in the absence of supplementary legislation). For those corporations to which it would apply, the bill (as revised in March 1969) defines principal as "not less than the fair value of the fund or other real or personal property at the time it was received by the corporation," while "the income thereof may include so much of the realized appreciation of principal as the board may deem prudent." S. 956A §513(d) (N.Y. 1969-1970). Adjustments and the establishment of reserves on account of changes in the purchasing power of the dollar would thus be left to the discretion of the board.

Can a statute which defines the appreciation of endowment funds as income be applied retroactively to gifts received prior to its enactment, or must it be applied only prospectively to future gifts? Whether the rule is promulgated by statute or by judicial decision, there is no substantial authority to be found in law or reason for denying it retroactive application.

When the Uniform Principal and Income Act was adopted it changed the apportionment of some items of revenue between principal and income. It was argued that the retroactive application of the statute to existing trusts would deprive either the income beneficiaries or the remaindermen of their property without due process of law. Professor Scott spoke for the overwhelming majority of commentators when he said:

> "[T]here should be no constitutional objection to making the Act retroactive. The rules as to allocation should not be treated as absolute rules of property law, but rather as rules as to the administration of the trust. The purpose is to make allocations which are fair and impartial as between the successive beneficiaries."[159]

All of the courts which considered the matter reached the same conclusion (although the Pennsylvania Supreme Court had to overrule an earlier decision to the contrary).[160]

There would be even less reason to deny retroactive application to an apportionment statute which dealt only with the endowment funds of educational institutions, because such a statute could not be said to deprive any beneficiary of vested property rights. The only argument which could be made against retroactivity for such a statute would be that it might violate the intent of the donor. Such an argument was also made in respect of the Uniform Principal and Income Act, but it was uniformly rejected by the courts. The language of a Minnesota case is typical:

> "[I]t is doubtful whether testatrix had any clear intention in mind at the time the will was executed. It is equally plausible that if she had thought about it at all she would have desired to have the dividends go where the law required them to go at the time they were received by the trustee . . . ."[161]

Use of Quasi-Endowment Funds: One of the primary benefits to be gained from the classification of realized gains as income is that it would make it practicable for many endowment fund managers, who now feel forced to invest in low-growth securities because of the pressing demands of their institutions for high current income, to seek instead the highest overall return from their investments through dividends, interest and gains combined. A practical alternative for obtaining that result without classifying gains as income is open to the many institutions with substantial capital funds which are not restricted as to the expenditure of principal. Under this approach, pioneered by Yale and the Museum of Modern Art, the institution determines the current return it can prudently demand from its investment portfolio, and to the extent that such a return cannot be met by dividends and interest, the deficit can be made up from the gains of the institution's quasi-endowment funds, or even from the principal (which can be expended in the institution's discretion). As already noted, a modified version of the practice has recently been adopted by Cornell and the University of Chicago, which now invest their endowment funds in comparatively conservative securities, and their quasi-endowment funds in more speculative, growth-oriented stocks.*

An important advantage offered by this approach is that it is available for use now, without the necessity of waiting for a declaratory judgment or legislation. Among its disadvantages is the fact that it can be employed as a practical matter only by institutions fortunate enough to possess a substantial amount of investment funds the principal of which they are free to spend. Our survey of educational institutions with investment funds in excess of $3 million indicated that 26% of the responding institutions have less than $500,000 of quasi-endowment funds or none at all. The practice is also subject to the criticism that it forces the institutions to do indirectly what they should have the right to do directly.** But the most important disadvantage of the approach is that it forces the institutions to deplete their most flexible, and therefore their most valued, assets. And if those assets do not appreciate rapidly enough to compensate for this new demand upon them, the solution will necessarily be short-term.

Donative Instruments: Looking to the future, another avenue to greater flexibility in the administration of college and university endowment funds is the wording of suggested forms of donative instruments. Most institutions make such forms available for the guidance of prospective donors, and if their terminology were improved the institutions might well reap the benefit of increased flexibility in endowment administration over a period of years, as the funds governed by such terminology multiply. It should be recognized, however, that such a process is of course gradual and would leave untouched the billions of dollars in existing educational endowments. For this reason changes in the wording

---

*See p. 41, *supra*.

**The same criticism can be levelled with equal justification at our proposal to utilize realized gains, as distinguished from unrealized appreciation. See pp. 34-35, *supra*.

of future donative instruments, although important and worthy of the most careful consideration, nevertheless offer the least prospect of dramatic improvement in flexibility of any of the avenues discussed in this report.

The gift which provides the ultimate in flexibility, and therefore the one which is most useful and most highly valued, is the gift which is completely unrestricted as to the purpose for which it may be used and as to the expenditure of principal.[162] The simplest of donative terminology will suffice:

> "I hereby give [or devise or bequeath] the sum of $_____
> [or property or securities, to be described] to _____
> University, to be used in such manner as it may choose *for any of its general purposes.*"*

But many donors prefer to establish or contribute to a permanent fund which will continue to benefit the institution indefinitely. For such donors the following language is suggested for gifts of money:

> "I hereby give [or bequeath] the sum of $_____ to
> _____ University, to be invested and reinvested as it may choose, separately or together with other funds of the University, without restriction to any statutory list of permissible investments. The principal of this gift shall be held in perpetuity, and the income, including** so much of the appreciation as the University may deem prudent, may be used in such manner as it may choose *for any of its general purposes.*"***

If the donation consists of property or securities, the first sentence of the last paragraph could be changed to read as follows:

> "I hereby give [or devise or bequeath] [property or securities, to be described] to _____ University, to be retained or liquidated in whole or in part as it may choose, the proceeds to be invested or reinvested as it may choose, separately or together with other funds of the University, without restriction to any statutory list of permissible investments."

---

*If the donor wishes to specify the purpose for which the gift is to be used, an appropriate substitution may be made for the italicized words, such as "for the payment of faculty salaries."

**We suggest that income be defined as *including* appreciation, rather than providing for the expenditure of appreciation *in addition to* or *together with* income. Use of the latter phrasing could be considered a representation by the institution that income alone does not include appreciation.

***An appropriate substitution may be made for the italicized words, if the donor wishes to specify the purpose for which the gift can be used.

II
Other Legal Problems
Affecting Endowment Funds

Thus far in this report we have concentrated on the treatment of endowment fund appreciation. There are other aspects of the law which have a bearing on the formulation of sound investment policies, however, and in the space remaining we shall turn our attention to several such areas.

Permissible Investments: We have seen that endowment fund managers may as a practical matter be restricted in their choice of investments because of the pressing need of their institutions for current revenue. Restrictions on permissible investments can also be imposed directly, by donors or by the legislature.

To determine the extent to which donors restrict the freedom of donee institutions to invest in securities of their choice, an analysis was made of the donative instruments which have been discussed earlier in this report.* Very few restrictions were found; most of the instruments do not even touch upon the question of permissible investments.**

Five of the 462 instruments, covering about 1½% of the aggregate value of the funds studied, contain some explicit restrictions on the type of investments the institutions are permitted to make. Two of these were gifts of stock which had not been registered under the Securities Act of 1933, and to avoid a public offering the donor required the institutions to obtain the donor's permission prior to transferring the stock within five years of the date of the gift. Two others contain restrictions only in the very broadest sense ("to be invested in income-producing securities"). Only one contains truly restrictive provisions on permitted investments.

Twenty-four instruments, covering approximately 3% of the aggregate value of the funds involved, use formal trust language in describing the gift.*** From this it might be inferred, in states which have a statu-

---

*See pp. 9-12 and 35-37, *supra*.

**There are times when an institution feels constrained to retain in its portfolio a specific investment as a matter of good donor-relations, as for example when the donor's gift consists of stock of a company in which he is particularly interested. While such constraints pose a practical problem, we are here concerned only with restrictions explicitly set forth in the donative instrument itself or fairly implied from the terms thereof.

***When the instruments were analyzed to determine restrictions placed by donors on the expenditure of principal, instruments covering 5% rather than 3% of the aggregate value of the funds involved were classified in this category. (See p. 10, *supra*.) Apparent discrepancies such as this in the results of the different analyses arise because the same instrument may fall within several of the classifications used. In such a case the instrument has been placed in the classification which most closely fits the donor's explicit instructions. If several classifications seem equally plausible, the most restrictive has been used. To illustrate, a number of instruments which used trust language went on explicitly to give the donee institutions complete control over the type of investments, but were silent as to the expenditure or maintenance of principal. Such instruments were classified in the "trust" category in the analysis relating to the expenditure of principal, but were classified in the "complete freedom" category in the analysis relating to permissible investments.

tory legal list of permitted investments for trustees, that the donor intended the institution to be governed by such legal list in the investment of the fund. Similarly, a small number of instruments, covering about one-half of one per cent of the aggregate value of the funds, speak of "interest" arising from investment. From this it could be argued that the donor intended his gift to be invested only in interest-bearing securities and not in stock.*

The great bulk of instruments, covering 95% of the aggregate value of the funds studied, contain no restrictions on permissible investments. Of these, instruments covering approximately 5% of the aggregate value of the funds studied specifically give the donee institutions complete discretion over investments.

Turning to the law, we find that most states have statutes dealing with the subject of permissible investments. Relatively few of these relate only to educational institutions,[163] a slightly larger number relate to non-profit corporations generally,[164] and most relate to "trustees" and "other fiduciaries."[165] A few states have statutes in all three categories. For example, New York grants to the trustees of every educational corporation chartered by the Board of Regents the power to "buy, sell, mortgage, let and otherwise use and dispose of its property as they shall deem for the best interests of the institution . . . ."[166] As to non-profit corporations generally, a New York statute provides that

> "Subject to the limitations and conditions contained in any gift, devise or bequest, a membership corporation . . . may invest its funds in such mortgages, bonds, debentures, shares of preferred and common stock and other securities as its directors shall deem advisable . . . ."[167]

By contrast, "fiduciaries" are subject to a legal list of permissible investments for "trust funds" managed by them, but may invest up to 50% of the aggregate market value of the funds in "other securities of corporations," provided that all corporate stocks selected for investment are listed on a national securities exchange.[168] The terms "fiduciary" and "trust" are so defined that they would only apply to funds subject to an express trust "for the benefit of a named or otherwise described income or principal beneficiary, or both."[169]

Most statutes which specifically apply to educational institutions or to non-profit corporations generally permit the institution to exercise

---

*No case was found in which such an inference was drawn, and in the absence of more explicit language it seems unlikely that a court would so construe such instruments.

wide discretion in the investment of its funds. For example, California grants to non-profit corporations all the powers

> "of control, management, investment, change, and disposal incident to the absolute ownership of property or funds by a private person, subject only to the terms of particular trusts and to the general trust that all its properties and funds shall be held for charitable and eleemosynary purposes."[170]

Pennsylvania and Tennessee permit directors of non-profit corporations, including educational institutions, to invest

> "in such investments as in the honest exercise of their judgment they may, after investigation, determine to be safe and proper investments, and to retain any investments heretofore so made."[171]

A number of states have adopted the Model Non-Profit Corporation Act, which gives such corporations unlimited power to invest in

> "shares or other interests in, or obligations of, other domestic or foreign corporations, whether for profit or not for profit, associations, partnerships or individuals, or direct or indirect obligations of the United States, or of any other government, state, territory, governmental district or municipality or of any instrumentality thereof."[172]

West Virginia applies the classic Prudent Man Rule to educational institutions. This requires the trustees of the institution to

> "exercise the judgment and care under the circumstances then prevailing which men of prudence, discretion and intelligence exercise in the management of their own affairs, not in regard to speculation, but in regard to the permanent disposition of their funds, considering the probable income as well as the probable safety of their capital."[173]

Where the statute prescribes investment standards for "trustees" and "fiduciaries," it is a question of interpretation whether the standards are meant to apply to educational institutions.[174] In more than half the states the statutory standard is the Prudent Man Rule.[175] That is the test almost always applied by courts today in the absence of a legislative pronouncement of some other standard, and it therefore makes little practical difference in such states whether the statute applies or not.[176] A problem arises only where the statute limits fiduciaries to a "legal list" of permitted investments.* The Restatement takes the flat position

---

*Consider also the archaic prescription imposed by the Montana constitution:
> "Art. V, § 37. No act of the legislative assembly shall authorize the investment of trust funds by executors, administrators, guardians or trustees in the bonds or stock of any private corporation."

that such statutes do not apply to charitable corporations,[177] a view which is supported by the scant authority in point.[178]

Where the applicable standard is the Prudent Man Rule, it should be remembered that the prudence demanded is that which is called for "under the circumstances then prevailing."[179] As was noted in a recent article:

> "The quality of prudence doesn't change but what is prudent does change. The prudent man is the prudent man of his time and the wording of the Prudent Man Rule must be taken in the context of the time of the investment. What may have been prudent in 1865 might well not be prudent in 1965 . . . ."[180]

In today's inflationary economy prudence demands that an attempt be made to safeguard the purchasing power of capital, as well as its original dollar value. As the author of the foregoing article went on to state:

> "Probably the risk to be minimized in the original concept of prudence was the risk of dollar loss. But in today's atmosphere of seemingly inevitable inflation and of actual pressure on the dollar from outside sources and the possibility of actual devaluation, the risk to be minimized might well be the risk of only having maintained the actual dollar value of trust principal."[181]

The author noted that while no court has yet surcharged a trustee for failure to seek the appreciation of a trust res, the possibility of such a holding in light of current financial trends is by no means remote.

In summary, donors, legislatures and the common law alike have as a rule given educational institutions wide discretion in the choice of investments. The requirement most frequently applied is that the institution invest as a prudent man would invest his own funds for the long term, having in mind both income and the safety of capital. Today capital cannot be considered safe unless its purchasing power is protected.

The Fear of Liability: Those investments with the greatest possibility of appreciation are generally those which entail the greatest risk of loss. If one chooses a common stock instead of a bond, one gains the possibility of growth but only at the risk of loss. Granted that the directors of educational institutions generally have wide discretion in choosing investments, what if their choice is wrong? Under what circumstances will they be liable?

If the jurisdiction has enacted statutory guidelines for the investment of funds of charitable corporations, directors will be liable for losses suffered by the corporations because of the failure of the directors to follow the guidelines. A few statutes specifically provide for such liability.[182] But as we have seen, few of the statutes applicable to charitable corporations offer guidelines any more specific than the Prudent Man Rule. To ascertain the standards under which liability will be imposed we therefore must turn to the decisions of the courts. And because of the paucity of cases dealing with charitable corporations, we turn first to trusts and business corporations.

Here as in so many other areas the law of trusts and the law of corporations offer divergent answers. Both of them start with the standard of prudence,[183] but they apply it differently.[184] The trustee is held to a comparatively strict standard. He is liable for losses resulting from his negligence[185] and even for losses "resulting from his failure to use the care and skill of a man of ordinary prudence, although he may have exercised all the care and skill of which he was capable."[186] However, even the liability of a trustee has reasonable limitations:

> "A trustee is liable for losses resulting from his failure to use the requisite care, skill or caution; but he is not a guarantor or an insurer nor liable for surcharge for shrinkage of value due to economic conditions over which he had no control.
>
> "A trustee is not required to be infallible in his judgment or anticipatory of events which were not generally anticipated...."[187]

The courts are more lenient with the directors of business corporations. As Hornstein notes in Corporation Law and Practice:

> " 'Mere' negligence . . . which would subject a trustee to liability, is not adjudged as serious a deficiency in a director. More is required before the latter is held to account in a situation where he is not charged with personal profit."[188]

Professor Ballantine doubts that more is required of directors than reasonable attention to the business, the making of proper inquiries and the exercise of honest judgment, unless improvidence goes to the point of "wilful or negligent waste."[189] And a review of the cases in which liability has actually been imposed on directors fully supports the conclusion reached by Professor Bishop in 1968:

> "I remain very skeptical of the proposition that directors of industrial corporations run any substantial risk of liability for ordinary negligence. There is, in fact, little precedent for liability even for the kind of Merovingian supineness for which directors were held liable in the old bank cases."[190]

As one might expect, there is a diversity of opinion as to the liability of directors of charitable corporations. Some commentators, observing that such directors are public-spirited citizens who usually serve without compensation, urge that they be held to a standard of care even lower than that imposed on business directors.[191] The courts make the same point without necessarily subscribing to a lower standard. For example, a Nebraska court noted that charitable directors serve without pay and are called upon for "unselfish, civic-minded service of men of high integrity, experience, and training in the investment and administration of large sums of money." However, the standard of liability announced by the court was substantially a reiteration of the Prudent Man Rule.[192] A Massachusetts court refused to remove charitable directors who diversified their holdings by selling stock at a loss, thereby missing substantial appreciation which occurred after the sale. The court conceded that "as events turned out, they did not sell the stock at the most propitious time, [but that] does not justify their removal; otherwise there would be few, if any, who would undertake to act as trustees."[193]

A few commentators have gone to the other extreme and urged that charitable directors be held to the liability of strict trustees.[194] But the weight of authority supports the conclusion of the Supreme Court of Minnesota:

> "The trustees of a charitable corporation, as members of its managing body, are charged with the same fidelity in the performance of functional duty as the directors of a private business corporation. . . ."[195]

Very few cases have dealt with the specific issue of the liability of charitable directors for investment losses. Perhaps the best known arose in California, where the founder of a charitable corporation who served as its president and a director caused it to engage in negligent and speculative investment, leading to a loss of $3,000,000. Successor directors brought suit against the founder and other former directors, but the court refused to impose personal liability, apparently because of the absence of bad faith. The court purported to apply a strict trust standard of accountability, but it was clearly something lower than that:

> "Assuming that the alleged losses were due to the alleged egregious blunders of the board under the leadership of President Pepperdine, and to have been the result of his negligence and of the lack of zealous interest on the part of the others, why should he be now required to restore to his corporation what he once gave from his bounty and which was lost solely by reason of his ignorant or careless reckoning? Although a director of such a corporation is held to the highest degree of honor and integrity, he is not personally liable for mistake of judgment."[196]

Trust standards were also ostensibly applied in a well known Arkansas case, where the finance committee of a college had authorized the treasurer to borrow $15,000 from endowment to pay debts of the college. The Supreme Court treated the transaction as an investment of funds which was reasonable under the circumstances, stressing that the committee members' "honesty of purpose is not questioned."[197]

Perhaps the clearest statement of the standards which govern the conduct of the directors of charitable corporations appears in a decision of the United States Court of Appeals for the 10th Circuit:

> "The directors of a corporation are charged with the duty of managing its affairs honestly and in good faith, and they must exercise ordinary and reasonable care in the performance of their duties. They must act with fidelity to the interests of the corporation, and they are jointly and severally liable for losses of the corporation proximately resulting from bad faith, fraudulent breaches of trust, or gross or wilful negligence in the discharge of their duties. But under the law of Kansas the directors of a corporation, acting in good faith and within the limitations of the law, have the power to determine its policies and manage its affairs. . . . And ill-success or bad judgment not so reckless or extravagant as to amount to bad faith or gross or wilful negligence on the part of directors in the discharge of their duties do not warrant the appointment of a receiver for the corporation or the rendition of a personal judgment against the directors."[198]

In summary, neither directors nor trustees are liable under the law for reasonable mistakes of judgment or for failure to foresee events which are not generally anticipated. A trustee may be liable for actual negligence, but directors have not even been held to that standard. As a practical matter the courts require proof of bad faith or gross or wilful neglect before imposing personal liability upon directors of business corporations, and the little authority in point indicates that this is true also in respect of directors of charitable corporations.

Delegation of Investment Responsibility: In view of the enormous size of college and university endowment funds, the intricacies of the market and the complexities of the economy, it seems obvious that management of the funds calls for professional skill and careful, day-to-day attention.[199] The boards of directors of most educational institutions are simply not equipped to make investment decisions on a daily basis. As the treasurer of one large university recently observed:

> ". . . since they [the directors] cannot attend continuously to the administration of this responsibility, there must be a Finance Committee; and since it, too, cannot be in continuous session, it

must have a Chairman; and since the Chairmanship is not, and should not be, the whole life work of the Chairman, there must be a professional adviser. Moreover, it is now generally agreed among experts that to achieve the best results the professional adviser must have sufficient competence to assume real responsibility for investment performance, and to lead in regard to transactions. Ordinarily, protracted Committee consideration of particular investments should be unnecessary. Indeed, the best modern portfolio managers cannot be employed on any other basis."[200]

According to a 1967 survey, most of the leading educational institutions accept and follow this view.[201] It thus appears that the directors of educational institutions delegate investment responsibilities at least to some extent, and as a practical matter they must do so. To what extent does the law sanction such delegation, and how far can it go?

A trustee, whether of a private or charitable trust, is under a duty not to delegate "acts which the trustee can reasonably be required personally to perform."[202] Specifically, he cannot delegate the "power to select investments," although he may solicit advice, particularly if it concerns "professional skills or facilities . . . not possessed by the trustee himself."[203] The directors of a business corporation, on the other hand, operate under modern statutes which permit the delegation of most board functions to executive committees.[204] Beyond this, the board "may delegate to subordinate officers and agents the authority to act for and represent the corporation, even in matters involving the exercise of judgment and discretion,"[205] although the board remains obligated to supervise corporate affairs.[206] The difference between the trustee and the corporate board, while in one sense merely one of degree, is nevertheless crucial from the standpoint of effective daily operations. Both have a fiduciary obligation, but the trustee must make the actual decision while the board may delegate that responsibility and merely exercise general supervisory powers.

The Model Non-Profit Corporation Act places the responsibility for the management of the corporation on the board of directors.[207] The board may delegate most of its duties to committees composed of two or more directors (without, however, relieving the board of its ultimate responsibility), and may also exercise the corporate power to "elect or appoint officers and agents of the corporation . . . and define their duties."[208] Many states have adopted statutes which follow this general pattern.[209] The Second Restatement of Trusts states that while a trustee may not delegate investment responsibilities, a distinction should be drawn in the case of charitable corporations:

> "It may be proper, for example, for the board [of a charitable corporation] to appoint a committee of its members to deal with the investment of the funds of the corporation, the board merely exercising a general supervision over the actions of the committee."[210]

If it is legally permissible for the full board of directors to delegate investment responsibility to a committee of its members, the next question posed is whether such responsibility may properly be delegated to a responsible officer of the corporation. It is submitted that the law should recognize that such delegation is a practical necessity for many educational institutions.[211]

From a logical standpoint, whatever method a corporation may choose to administer its funds, it clearly must act through agents. This is true even of corporate trustees. And as the business of the corporation grows more complex, more and more of the acts of the corporation must be performed by agents other than directors. When a bank or trust company is named as a trustee, no one expects its board of directors to make the investment decisions for each of the trusts it administers. That is the function of trust officers who may be fairly far down in the corporate hierarchy. Similarly, the part-time, unpaid directors of educational institutions should not be expected personally to make the decisions to buy and sell the securities in multi-million dollar portfolios.

Technically, the principle that trustees may not delegate investment responsibility has nothing to do with delegation within a corporate structure, even when the corporation is a technical trustee. In such a case the trustee itself delegates nothing; it acts through agents, as it must. Professor Scott points out that the underlying reason for the rule against delegation, "the element of reliance upon personal judgment and discretion[,] is wanting in the case of a corporate trustee, since it can act only through its directors, officers and employees and these may change from time to time."[212] Without reference to investment responsibility he states that certain acts are of sufficient importance that they must be performed by the directors or by a responsible committee or officer and not by an ordinary employee. This is of course true also in the case of a business corporation. It is based on the logical operation of the corporate chain of command and not upon technicalities of trust law.

The courts have very rarely dealt with the delegation of investment responsibility by charitable corporations. When they have they seem to have approved it. In Massachusetts, a charitable corporation by a by-law established a trust fund which was to receive all general donations to the corporation and use the income for the charitable purposes of the corporation. For fifty-six years the fund was managed by trustees who were not necessarily members of the corporate board. In 1947 the Massachusetts Supreme Judicial Court said that these trustees were "officers and agents of the corporation and constantly subject to its control," and indicated that this procedure was both regular and lawful.[213]

A Pennsylvania case involved a gift which had been made in trust to the City of Philadelphia, to be administered by the commissioners of a certain park. The court found the following method of managing investments to be "most satisfactory":

> "The purchase and sale of all securities is supervised by a special committee, of which [the treasurer of the commission, a highly regarded financial expert] is a member. The committee keeps full minutes of its deliberations and reviews the trust portfolio at frequent intervals. Experts in various branches of the investment business are invited to sit with the committee. Between meetings the list of investments held by the estate is submitted to various investment bankers, for review and suggestions. All of the securities are presently held by the Philadelphia National Bank, as custodian."[214]

It is not clear whether the committee was composed of commissioners, but it was clearly something less than the full commission.*

Although it used trust law as a guide, an Arkansas court raised no issue of delegation in approving an investment made by members of a college finance committee.[216] It does not appear from the opinion where the committee stood in the hierarchy of the college structure. And a Connecticut court refused to remove trustees of a school or hold them liable for losses resulting from the mismanagement of funds which they had turned over to a lawyer and real estate agent of good reputation for investment.[217]

The last-mentioned case raises another problem. Thus far we have limited our discussion to delegation within the corporate structure. As we pointed out above, such delegation should be allowed even if strict trust law were applied to the administration of educational endowment funds, because the "trustee" (the educational institution) in fact delegates nothing. A different question is presented when the power to make

---

*The court also noted that the trustee is the city and not the commission or the individual commissioners. For that reason no accountings were required upon a change in personnel of the commissioners. The court observed that this was equally true in respect of the officers and directors of eleemosynary institutions.[215]

64

investment decisions and act upon them is delegated to an adviser or manager outside the corporation.

Even under corporate law, directors are forbidden to abdicate their responsibility to manage the affairs of the corporation.[218] In the absence of statute it is unlikely that the courts would condone a complete surrender of investment responsibility to outsiders.* But *some* use of outside investment counsel is clearly permissible. Even trustees are permitted to seek professional advice.[221] And it is submitted that there is no logical reason why a charitable corporation should not be free to enter into an arrangement with outside investment counsel pursuant to which the counsel makes the actual decision to buy and sell, providing that the corporation is kept currently informed of the decisions made and has the right to terminate the arrangement at any time.** Dangers could be minimized and objections obviated by the use of a reasonably select list of securities approved in advance by the corporation, from which the counsel is authorized to make new commitments in his discretion. Another safeguard might take the form of reasonable dollar limitations on the individual and aggregate commitments and eliminations which the counsel could undertake without advance approval. The essential point is that the person charged with investment responsibility, whether inside or outside the corporate structure, should be allowed sufficient freedom of action to enable him to exercise his independent judgment, while information is reported through the chain of command on a sufficiently current basis to enable the directors to discharge their duty to supervise corporate affairs.

In summary, there is nothing in the law to condemn the delegation of investment responsibility to a committee of the board and even to a responsible officer of a charitable corporation. Delegation outside the corporate structure can more easily be questioned, but such delegation should nevertheless be upheld if the corporation retains ultimate control.

---

*California has such a statute. It permits non-profit corporations to delegate investment authority in whole or in part to trust companies or banks.[219] A similar statute has recently been proposed by the Joint Legislative Committee to Study Revision of Corporation Laws for adoption in New York.[220]

**Informal discussions with educational institutions indicate that this is in fact the procedure followed by a number of them. It is also the common practice of investment companies. Investment advisory contracts entered into by such companies are required by statute to be terminable without penalty on not more than sixty days' notice.[222]

Conclusion

If the managers of educational endowment funds are being hampered in their efforts to develop sound investment policies, the fault cannot fairly be said to lie in the law. Legal impediments which have been thought to deprive managers of their freedom of action appear on analysis to be more legendary than real.

If the managers of endowment funds wish to seek long-term appreciation in their investments, the need of their institutions for current yield should not dissuade them. We find no authoritative support in the law for the widely held view that the realized gains of endowment funds can never be spent. Prudence would call for the retention of sufficient gains to maintain purchasing power in the face of inflation and to guard against potential losses, but subject to the standards which prudence dictates, the expenditure of gains should lie within the discretion of the institution's directors.

The law allows the managers of endowment funds wide latitude in their choice of investments, and no conscientious director need fear liability for an honest mistake of judgment. The administration of the fund can be handled within the corporate structure by the persons best suited to the task, and it would seem that outside investment counsel can be given wide responsibility for investment decisions, provided that the institution's directors do not abdicate their power of supervision.

Anglo-American law has never stood for long in the path of progress, but has accommodated to changing needs. This is and should be its role and function in the field of education.

Notes

1. Quoted in FINANCING HIGHER EDUCATION: 1960-70, at 9 (D. Keezer ed. 1959).
2. *See, e.g.,* HARVARD UNIVERSITY, THE UNIVERSITY AND ITS RESOURCES 15 (undated).
3. S. HARRIS, HIGHER EDUCATION: RESOURCE AND FINANCE 423-24 (1962); FINANCING HIGHER EDUCATION: 1960-70, at 67-68 (D. Keezer ed. 1959); 5 PRESIDENT'S COMMISSION ON HIGHER EDUCATION, HIGHER EDUCATION FOR AMERICAN DEMOCRACY, FINANCING HIGHER EDUCATON 31 (1947); M. Chambers, FINANCING HIGHER EDUCATION 4 (1963) (unpublished manuscript); *Report of the Treasurer for 1966-67,* BULL. OF YALE U. 15-16 (1968).
4. S. HARRIS, HIGHER EDUCATION: RESOURCE AND FINANCE 445-46 (1962); FINANCING HIGHER EDUCATION: 1960-70, at 68 (D. Keezer ed. 1959).
5. OFFICE OF EDUCATION, U.S. DEP'T OF HEALTH, EDUCATION & WELFARE, COLLEGE AND UNIVERSITY ENDOWMENT 8 (1965).
6. *Bonds vs. Stocks—Growing Dilemma,* 63 U.S. NEWS & WORLD REPORT, Dec. 18, 1967, at 87, 89.
7. S. HARRIS, HIGHER EDUCATION: RESOURCE AND FINANCE 424 (1962).
8. Matthew 25:14-30.
9. 2 AMERICAN COUNCIL ON EDUCATION, COLLEGE AND UNIVERSITY BUSINESS ADMINISTRATION 107 (1955); S. HARRIS, HIGHER EDUCATION IN THE UNITED STATES: THE ECONOMIC PROBLEMS 203, 204 (1960); S. HARRIS, HIGHER EDUCATION: RESOURCE & FINANCE 428 (1962); Buek, *Investments,* 29 COLLEGE & U. BUS., Oct. 1960, at 43; *Stocks-What the Experts Buy,* 64 U.S. NEWS & WORLD REPORT, March 4, 1968, at 58.
10. S. HARRIS, HIGHER EDUCATION IN THE UNITED STATES: THE ECONOMIC PROBLEMS 205 (1960).
11. *Norvell Estate,* 415 Pa. 427, 433, 203 A.2d 538, 542 (1964).
12. Blackwell, *Proper Utilization of Endowment Income,* 23 COLLEGE & U. BUS., Sept. 1957, at 53.
13. 3 SCOTT, LAW OF TRUSTS § 236.3 (3d ed. 1967).
14. *Jordan Est.,* 2 Fiduc. Rep. 561 (Pa. Orphan's Ct. 1952).
15. Quoted in Scott, *Education and the Dead Hand,* 34 HARV. L. REV. 1, 13-14 (1920).
16. S. HARRIS, HIGHER EDUCATION IN THE UNITED STATES: THE ECONOMIC PROBLEMS 205 (1960); Blackwell, *supra* note 12; Lincoln, *A Question on Gifts to Charitable Corporations,* 25 VA. L. REV. 764, 795 (1939).
17. Scott, *supra* note 15, at 14-15.
18. *St. Joseph's Hosp. v. Bennett,* 281 N.Y. 115, 118, 22 N.E.2d 305, 306 (1939).
19. IND. ANN. STAT. § 25-3202 (1960).
20. N.J. STAT. ANN. § 3A:14A (1952).
21. *See* 3 SCOTT, LAW OF TRUSTS § 236.14 (3d ed. 1967).
22. N.Y. PERS. PROP. LAW § 27-e (McKinney 1965), re-enacted in N.Y. ESTATES, POWERS & TRUSTS LAW § 11-2.1(e)(7) (McKinney 1967).
23. *Catherwood Trust,* 405 Pa. 61, 173 A.2d 86 (1961).
24. *Waterhouse's Est.,* 308 Pa. 422, 429, 162 A. 295, 296 (1932).
25. Note, *Allocation of Stock Dividends Between the Life Beneficiary and Remainderman,* 1966 WASH. U.L.Q. 216, 222 (1966).
26. *See, e.g.,* N.Y. ESTATES, POWERS & TRUSTS LAW § 11-2.1(k) (McKinney 1967); RESTATEMENT (SECOND) OF TRUSTS § 241 (1959); 3 SCOTT, LAW OF TRUSTS § 241.1 (3d ed. 1967).
27. UNIFORM PRINCIPAL & INCOME ACT § 3(b) (revised 1962 act); UNIFORM PRINCIPAL & INCOME ACT § 1 (1931).
28. Quoted in Staver, *The Uniform Principal and Income Act,* 21 ORE. L. REV. 217, 224 (1942).
29. Boylan, *Endowment Funds—Collision of Corporate and Trust Standards,* 18 BUS. LAW. 807 (1963).
30. Karst, *The Efficiency of the Charitable Dollar: An Unfulfilled State Responsibility,* 73 HARV. L. REV. 433, 435 (1960).
31. Boylan, *supra* note 29, at 807; *see* Karst, *supra* note 30, at 435.
32. Boylan, *supra* note 29, at 808.
33. *E.g., Loats Asylum v. Essom,* 220 Md. 11, 150 A.2d 742 (1958); *St. Joseph's Hosp. v.*

Bennett, 281 N.Y. 115, 22 N.E.2d 305 (1939); *Robert v. Corning*, 89 N.Y. 225 (1882); *Wetmore v. Parker*, 52 N.Y. 450 (1873); *see Estate of Berry*, 29 Wis.2d 506, 139 N.W.2d 72 (1966), which places Wisconsin in the New York camp although previously, in *Maxcy v. Oshkosh*, 144 Wis. 238, 128 N.W. 899 (1910), it looked to the donor's intent. *See also Schaeffer v. Newberry*, 235 Minn. 282, 50 N.W.2d 477 (1951), and *Lane v. Eaton*, 69 Minn. 141, 71 N.W. 1031 (1897), which indicate Minnesota for many years followed New York. *See* 4 SCOTT, LAW OF TRUSTS § 348.1 (3d ed. 1967); Blackwell, *The Charitable Corporation and the Charitable Trust*, 24 WASH. U.L.Q. 1, 13-21 (1938).

34. *E.g., Carter v. Mayor & City Council*, 197 Md. 70, 78 A.2d 212 (1951); *In re Durand*, 194 N.Y. 477, 87 N.E. 677 (1909).

35. *St. Joseph's Hosp. v. Bennett*, 281 N.Y. 115, 22 N.E.2d 305 (1939); *Wetmore v. Parker*, 52 N.Y. 450 (1873).

36. 4 SCOTT, LAW OF TRUSTS § 348.3 (3d ed. 1967).

37. *E.g., Bascom v. Albertson*, 34 N.Y. 584 (1 Redf.) 340 (1866); *see* 4 SCOTT, LAW OF TRUSTS § 348.3 (3d ed. 1967); Blackwell, *The Charitable Corporation and the Charitable Trust*, 24 WASH. U.L.Q. 1, 13-20 (1938).

38. *Bird v. Merklee*, 144 N.Y. 544, 550, 39 N.E. 645, 646-47 (1895).

39. *E.g., Lyme High School Ass'n v. Alling*, 113 Conn. 200, 154 A. 439 (1931); *Pierce v. Phelps*, 75 Conn. 83, 52 A. 612 (1902); *In re Myra Fnd.*, 112 N.W.2d 522 (N.D. 1961).

40. 4 SCOTT, LAW OF TRUSTS § 348.3 (3d ed. 1967).

41. *Crane v. Morristown School Fnd.*, 120 N.J. Eq. 583, 187 A. 632 (E. & A. 1936); *Montclair Nat'l Bank & Trust Co. v. Seton Hall Coll. of Med.*, 90 N.J. Super. 419, 217 A.2d 897 (Ch. 1966).

42. *E.g., Montclair Nat'l Bank & Trust Co. v. Seton Hall Col. of Med.*, 90 N.J. Super. 419, 217 A.2d 897 (Ch. 1966); *Bankers Trust Co. v. N. Y. Women's League for Animals*, 23 N.J. Super. 170, 92 A.2d 820 (App. Div. 1952).

43. *Hermosa Beach v. Superior Court*, 231 Cal. App. 2d 295, 299, 41 Cal. Rptr. 796, 799 (2d Dist. 1964).

44. *Orleans Parish School Bd. v. New Orleans*, 90 So. 2d 683, 688 (La. 1956).

45. *E.g., Hanover St. Presbyterian Church v. Buckson*, 210 A.2d 190 (Del. Ch. 1965); *Grear v. Sifford*, 289 Ill. App. 450, 7 N.E.2d 371 (4th Dist. 1937); *Zabel v. Stewart*, 153 Kan. 272, 109 P.2d 177 (1941); *Central Univ. v. Walters' Ex'rs*, 122 Ky. 65, 90 S.W. 1066 (1906); *Orleans Parish School Bd. v. New Orleans*, 90 So.2d 683 (La. 1956); *Whitmore v. Church of the Holy Cross*, 121 Me. 391, 117 A. 469 (1922); *Massachusetts Charitable Mechanic Ass'n v. Beede*, 320 Mass. 601, 70 N.E.2d 825 (1947); *Animal Rescue League v. Assessors*, 310 Mass. 330, 37 N.E.2d 1019 (1941); *Ohio Soc'y for Crippled Children & Adults v. McElroy*, 175 Ohio St. 49, 191 N.E. 2d 543 (1963). Although Wisconsin was at one time in this category, *Maxcy v. Oshkosh*, 144 Wis. 238, 128 N.W. 899 (1910), it now appears to have adopted the absolute ownership theory. *Estate of Berry*, 29 Wis.2d 506, 139 N.W.2d 72 (1966).

46. *Application of Mareck*, 257 Minn. 222, 100 N.W. 2d 758 (1960); *Clarke v. Sisters of the Soc'y of the Holy Child Jesus*, 82 Neb. 85, 117 N.W. 107 (1908).

47. *Trustees of Cumberland Univ. v. Caldwell*, 203 Ala. 590, 84 So. 846 (1919); *Perry v. Town of Friendship*,—Me.—, 237 A.2d 405 (1968); *Rohlff v. German Old People's Home*, 143 Neb. 636, 10 N.W.2d 686 (1943).

48. *E.g., Lovelace v. Marion Institute*, 215 Ala. 271, 110 So. 381 (1926).

49. *E.g., Peters v. East Penn Township School Dist.*, 182 Pa. Super. 116, 126 A.2d 802 (1956).

50. *E.g., Southwestern Presbyterian Univ. v. Clarksville*, 149 Tenn. 256, 259 S.W. 550 (1924).

51. *E.g., St. Joseph's Hosp. v. Bennett*, 281 N.Y. 115, 22 N.E.2d 305 (1939).

52. Note, *The Charitable Corporation*, 64 HARV. L. REV. 1168, 1173 (1951).

53. 1951 OP. ATT'Y GEN. 159, 161 (N.Y.)

54. RESTATEMENT (SECOND) OF TRUSTS § 389, comment b (1959); *see Yap v. Wah Yen Ki Tuk Tsen Nin Hue of Honolulu*, 43 Hawaii 37 (1958).

55. RESTATEMENT (SECOND) OF TRUSTS § 389, comment c (1959); *e.g.,* PA. STAT. ANN. tit. 15, § 7318 (1967); VT. STAT. ANN. tit. 16 § 3641 (1959). In its 1963 survey, the Department of Health, Education and Welfare found that 90% of all institutions surveyed pool their endowment funds for investment purposes. OFFICE OF EDUCATION, U.S. DEP'T OF HEALTH, EDUCATION & WELFARE, COLLEGE AND UNIVERSITY ENDOWMENT 54 n.2 (1965).

56. 11 W. FLETCHER, PRIVATE CORPORATIONS § 5325 (rev. vol. M. Wolf 1958).

57. 2 SCOTT, LAW OF TRUSTS § 182 (3d ed. 1967).

58. *Ibid.*

59. RESTATEMENT (SECOND) OF TRUSTS §§ 171, 379 (1959); 4 SCOTT, LAW OF TRUSTS § 379 (3d ed. 1967).

60. Boylan, *Endowment Funds—Collision of Corporate and Trust Standards*, 18 BUS. LAW. 807, 810 (1963); Welles, *University Endowments: Revolution Comes to the Ivory Tower*, 1 INSTITUTIONAL INVESTOR, Sept. 1967, at 11.

61. MODEL NON-PROFIT CORPORATION ACT §§ 17, 21 (rev. act 1964).

62. RESTATEMENT (SECOND) OF TRUSTS § 379, comment b (1959).

63. *Denckla v. Independence Fnd.*, 41 Del. Ch. 251, 193 A.2d 538, 541 (1963).
64. *Id.* at 252, 193 A.2d at 541.
65. *Id.* at 256, 193 A.2d at 544.
66. *Hospital & Benevolent Ass'n v. Baptist State Conv.*, 176 Ark. 946, 958, 4 S.W.2d 933, 937 (1928).
67. *Central Univ. v. Walters' Ex'rs*, 122 Ky. 65, 83, 90 S.W. 1066, 1070 (1906).
68. *E.g., People v. President & Trustees of the Col. of Cal.*, 38 Cal. 166 (1869); *Holden Hosp. Corp. v. Southern Illinois Hosp. Corp.*, 22 Ill.2d 150, 174 N.E.2d 793 (1961); *Trustees of Rush Med. Col. v. University of Chicago*, 312 Ill. 109, 143 N.E. 434 (1924); *Orleans Parish School Bd. v. New Orleans*, 90 So.2d 683 (La. 1956); *contra, Hempstead v. Meadville Theological School*, 284 Pa. 147, 130 A. 421 (1925).
69. *E.g., Trevathan v. Ringgold—Noland Fnd.*, 241 Ark. 758, 410 S.W.2d 132 (1967); *Lupton v. Leander Clark Col.*, 194 Iowa 1008, 187 N.W. 496 (1922); *President and Trustees of Harvard Col. v. Soc'y for Promoting Theological Ed.*, 69 Mass (3 Gray) 280 (1855); *Catron v. Scarritt Collegiate Inst.*, 264 Mo. 713, 175 S.W. 571 (1915); *Bible Readers' Aid Soc'y v. Katzenbach*, 97 N.J. Eq. 416, 128 A. 628 (Ch. 1925); *Matter of Syracuse Univ. (Heffron)*, 3 N.Y.2d 665, 148 N.E.2d 671, 171 N.Y.S.2d 545 (1958); *Fenn Col. v. Nance*, 4 Ohio Misc. 183, 210 N.E.2d 418 (C.P. Cuyahoga County 1965); *cf. Stone v. Inhabitants of Framingham*, 109 Mass. 303 (1872).
70. *American Inst. of Architects v. Attorney Gen.*, 332 Mass. 619, 620-22, 127 N.E.2d 161, 161-63 (1955). *See also* RESTATEMENT (SECOND) OF TRUSTS § 348, comment f (1959).
71. *Attorney Gen. v. Olson*, 346 Mass. 190, 191 N.E.2d 132 (1963); *In re Myra Fnd.*, 112 N.W.2d 552 (N.D. 1961); *Wilstach Est.*, 1 Pa. D. & C.2d 197 (1954); *Estate of Berry*, 29 Wis. 2d 506, 139 N.W.2d 72 (1966).
72. PA. STAT. ANN. tit. 20, § 320.753(a) (1950).
73. *Spoerl Est.*, 5 Pa. D. & C.2d 130 (Orphans' Ct. 1955).
74. J. TILT, LEGAL INCIDENTS TO THE INVESTMENT OF THE CORPORATE FUNDS OF CHARITABLE CORPORATIONS ORGANIZED UNDER THE LAWS OF THE STATE OF NEW YORK WITH COMPARATIVE ANALYSIS OF DECISIONAL AND STATUTORY LAW IN OTHER JURISDICTIONS OF THE UNITED STATES 25, March 1952 (unpublished thesis, Brooklyn Law School).
75. N.Y. SURROGATE'S COURT PROCEDURE ACT § 2309 (McKinney 1967).
76. RESTATEMENT (SECOND) OF TRUSTS § 348, comment f (1959).
77. 4 SCOTT, LAW OF TRUSTS § 348.1 (3d ed. 1967); *see* RESTATEMENT (SECOND) OF TRUSTS § 348, comment f (1959).
78. *Groome's Est.*, 337 Pa. 250, 11 A.2d 271 (1940); *see* Note, *The Charitable Corporation*, 64 HARV. L. REV. 1168, 1173 (1951).
79. *People's Bank v. St. Anthony's Catholic Church*, 109 N.Y. 512, 521-22, 17 N.E. 408, 410 (1888).
80. Note, *The Charitable Corporation*, 64 HARV. L. REV. 1168, 1173 (1951); *see Sisters of Charity of Incarnate Word v. Emery*, 144 La. 614, 81 So. 99 (1919); *Sherwood v. American Bible Soc'y*, 40 N.Y. 561 (1864).
81. *Leeds v. Harrison*, 9 N.J. 202, 211-12, 87 A.2d 713, 717 (1952).
82. *Leeds v. Harrison*, 9 N.J. 202, 87 A.2d 713 (1952); *accord, Blauert v. Schupmann*, 241 Minn. 428, 63 N.W.2d 578 (1954).
83. *Grace v. Grace Inst.*, 19 N.Y.2d 307, 313, 226 N.E.2d 531, 533 (1967).
84. *Watson's Est.*, 314 Pa. 179, 182, 170 A. 254, 255 (1934); *accord, In re Wanamaker Inst. of Indus.*, 36 Pa. D. & C. 406 (1939).
85. *Commonwealth v. Seventh Day Baptists*, 317 Pa. 358, 176 A. 17 (1935).
86. *Attorney Gen. v. Illinois Agri. Col.*, 85 Ill. 516 (1877).
87. *Paterson v. Paterson Gen. Hosp.*, 97 N.J. Super. 514, 518, 235 A.2d 487, 489 (1967).
88. *Southwestern Presbyterian Univ. v. Clarksville*, 149 Tenn. 256, 269, 259 S.W. 550, 554 (1923).
89. *Hanover St. Presbyterian Church v. Buckson*, 210 A.2d 190, 192 (Del. Ch. 1965). *See also Trustees of Peninsula Ann. Conf. v. N.Y. East Ann. Conf.*, 211 A.2d 588 (Del. 1965).
90. MODEL BUS. CORP. ACT ANN. § 2(k) (1960).
91. *Id.* § 2, comment ¶ 2.01 at 21.
92. *Randall v. Bailey*, 288 N.Y. 280, 43 N.E.2d 43 (1942).
93. N.Y. BUS. CORP. LAW § 102(a)(6) (McKinney 1963).
94. *Woodson v. Lee*, 73 N.M. 425, 389 P.2d 196 (1963); *Kingston v. Home Life Ins. Co.*, 11 Del. Ch. 258, 101 A. 898, *aff'd*, 11 Del. Ch. 428, 104 A. 25 (1917).
95. *National Newark & Essex Banking Co. v. Durant Motor Co.*, 124 N.J. Eq. 213, 218, 1 A.2d 316, 319 (Ch. 1938), *aff'd*, 125 N.J. Eq. 435, 5 A.2d 767 (Ch. 1939).
96. *Equitable Life Ass. Soc'y v. Union Pac. R.R.*, 212 N.Y. 360, 369, 106 N.E. 92, 94 (1914).
97. *E.g.,* R. MUSGRAVE, THE THEORY OF PUBLIC FINANCE 164-65 (1959); W. VICKREY, AGENDA FOR PROGRESSIVE TAXATION 6 (1947).
98. R. Haig, *The Concept of Income—Economic and Legal Aspects*, in FEDERAL INCOME TAX 1, 27 (R. Haig ed. 1921).
99. H. SIMONS, PERSONAL INCOME TAX 50 (1938).

100. Haig, *supra* note 98, at 10-11; SIMONS, *supra* note 99, at 82.
101. Haig, *supra* note 98, at 16; SIMONS, *supra* note 99, at 155.
102. INT. REV. CODE of 1954, §§ 61(a)(3), 1201(b).
103. *In re Alleghany Corp.*, 6 S.E.C. 960, 964 (1940).
104. Dunham, *Valuing Life Estates and Remainders,* 107 TRUSTS & EST. 13, 80 (1968).
105. Address by William G. Stott, Executive Vice President, Morgan Guaranty Trust Co., 36th International Conference of the Financial Executives Institute, Oct. 17, 1967, in MORGAN GUARANTY SURVEY, October, 1967; *Stocks vs. Bonds—Growing Dilemma,* 63 U.S. NEWS & WORLD REPORT, Dec. 18, 1967, at 87.
106. *Report of the Treasurer,* 1965-66, BULL. OF YALE U. (Dec. 15, 1966).
107. 63 U.S. NEWS & WORLD REPORT, *supra* note 103; address by James J. O'Brien, 16th Annual Conference of Southwest Foundations (1964).
108. *See* S. HARRIS, HIGHER EDUCATION IN THE UNITED STATES: THE ECONOMIC PROBLEMS 203 (1960).
109. HARRIS, *supra* note 108, at 204-05; OFFICE OF EDUCATION, U.S. DEP'T OF HEALTH, EDUCATION & WELFARE, COLLEGE AND UNIVERSITY ENDOWMENT 53 (1965).
110. HARRIS, *supra* note 108, at 204.
111. *See Report of the Committee on Financial and Investment Policies,* 57 AM. ECON. REV. 711 (1967); Seward, *Earned Surplus—Its Meaning and Use in the Model Business Corporation Act,* 38 VA. L. REV. 435, 440 (1952); Slawson, *Taxing as Ordinary Income the Appreciation of Publicly Held Stock,* 76 YALE L. J. 623 (1967).
112. *See* cases cited *supra* note 94.
113. *See* 3 SCOTT, LAW OF TRUSTS §§ 236.11, 236.12 (3d ed. 1967).
114. *Randall v. Bailey,* 288 N.Y. 280, 43 N.E.2d 43 (1942).
115. N.Y. BUS. CORP. L. § 102(a)(6) (McKinney 1963).
116. INT. REV. CODE of 1954, § 1201(b).
117. *See, e.g.,* Slawson, *Taxing as Ordinary Income the Appreciation of Publicly Held Stock,* 76 YALE L.J. 623 (1967).
118. OFFICE OF EDUCATION, U.S. DEP'T OF HEALTH, EDUCATION & WELFARE, COLLEGE AND UNIVERSITY ENDOWMENT 55 (1963).
119. 2 AMERICAN COUNCIL ON EDUCATION, COLLEGE AND UNIVERSITY BUSINESS ADMINISTRATION 126 (1955).
120. RESTATEMENT (SECOND) OF TRUSTS § 348, comment f (1959).
121. *See* statutes cited note 55, *supra.*
122. *See* RESTATEMENT (SECOND) OF TRUSTS § 389, comment c (1959).
123. *See* 11 W. FLETCHER, PRIVATE CORPORATIONS § 5325 (rev. vol. M. Wolf 1958).
124. 2 SCOTT, LAW OF TRUSTS § 182 (3d ed. 1967).
125. *Ibid.*
126. *See* 4 SCOTT, LAW OF TRUSTS § 348.1 (3d ed. 1967)
127. Mulreany, *Permissible Accumulations,* PROCEEDINGS OF THE SIXTH BIENNIAL CONFERENCE ON CHARITABLE FOUNDATIONS 157, 158 (1963).
128. Pasley, *Proposed Changes in the New York Statutes on Accumulations,* 46 CORNELL L.Q. 16, 31 (1960).
129. *Ibid.*
130. *Wardens, etc., of St. Paul's Church v. Attorney Gen.,* 164 Mass. 188, 41 N.E. 231 (1895).
131. *Webb v. Webb,* 340 Ill. 407, 172 N.E. 730 (1930); *Wardens, etc., of St. Paul's Church v. Attorney Gen.,* 164 Mass. 188, 41 N.E. 231 (1895); *Hartford Nat'l Bank & Trust Co. v. Billings P. Learned Missions,* 22 Conn. Supp. 409, 174 A.2d 49 (Super. Ct. 1961); *Brown v. Saake,* 190 So.2d 56 (Fla. Dist. Ct. App. 1966); *Schreiner v. Cincinnati Altenheim,* 61 Ohio App. 344, 22 N.E. 2d 587 (Ct. App. 1939).
132. RESTATEMENT OF PROPERTY § 439(a)(ii) (1944).
133. *Id.* at comment d.
134. *Schreiner v. Cincinnati Altenheim,* 61 Ohio App. 344, 22 N.E.2d 587 (Ct. App. 1939); BOGERT, THE LAW OF TRUSTS AND TRUSTEES § 217 (2d ed. 1965).
135. *See, e.g.,* N.Y. ESTATES, POWERS & TRUSTS LAW § 9-2.1(a) (McKinney 1967); PA. STAT. ANN. tit. 20, § 301.6(b)(1) (1950), *as amended* (Supp. 1967).
136. Pasley, *supra* note 128, at 47-49.
137. CAL. CORP. CODE § 10207 (West 1955).
138. Treas. Reg. § 1.504-1(c)(2) (1958).
139. INT. REV. CODE of 1954, § 503 (b)(2).
140. T. ARNETT, COLLEGE AND UNIVERSITY FINANCE 24-26 (1922); T. Blackwell, discussed in HARRIS, HIGHER EDUCATION IN THE UNITED STATES: THE ECONOMIC PROBLEMS 205 (1960); J. RUSSELL, THE FINANCE OF HIGHER EDUCATION 266 (rev. ed. 1954); Johns, *Accounting for Endowment Funds,* 10 COLLEGE & U. BUS., March 1951, at 25, 27.
141. *Authors Club v. Kirtland,* 248 App. Div. 82, 288 N.Y.S. 916 (1st Dep't 1936).
142. *Ibid; State ex rel. Crutze v. Toney,* 141 Ore. 406, 17 P.2d 1105 (1933).
143. *Matter of United Bd. for Christian Higher Ed. in Asia,* 159 N.Y.L.J., no. 39, p. 17, col. 1 (Sup. Ct. Feb. 27, 1968).

144. *Massachusetts Charitable Mechanic Ass'n v. Beede,* 320 Mass. 601, 70 N.E.2d 825 (1947).
145. *Hobbs v. Board of Ed.,* 126 Neb. 416, 253 N.W. 627 (1934).
146. ARNETT, *supra* note 140; RUSSELL, *supra* note 140, at 266-67; Johns, *supra* note 140.
147. 1951 OP. ATT'Y GEN. 159, 161 (N.Y.)
148. 1 HORNSTEIN, CORPORATION LAW AND PRACTICE § 446 (1959); *see* N.Y. BUS. CORP. LAW § 717 (McKinney 1963).
149. RESTATEMENT (SECOND) OF TRUSTS §§ 174 and 379 (1959).
150. WEBSTER'S NEW INTERNATIONAL DICTIONARY 1996 (2d ed. unabridged 1939).
151. *Report of the Treasurer, 1966-67,* BULL. OF YALE U. (Jan. 27, 1968); *Report of the Treasurer, 1965-66,* BULL. OF YALE U. (Dec. 15, 1966).
152. *Report of the Treasurer of Cornell, 1968* (Sept. 10, 1968); Office of Public Relations, University of Chicago, Press Release (March 5, 1968).
153. *Report of the Treasurer of Cornell, 1968,* p.2 (Sept. 10, 1968).
154. *Report of Committee on Financial and Investment Policies,* 57 AM. ECON. REV. 711 (1967).
155. OFFICE OF EDUCATION, *supra* note 118.
156. *Id.* at 30.
157. *See, e.g.,* M. FRIEDMAN & A. SCHWARTZ, A MONETARY HISTORY OF THE UNITED STATES, 1867-1960, chart 62 (1963).
158. 1 HORNSTEIN, *supra* note 148, at § 463; Bugge, *Unrealized Appreciation as a Source of Shareholder Distributions under the Wisconsin Business Corporation Law,* 1964 WIS. L. REV. 292, 298.
159. Scott, *Principal or Income?,* 100 TRUSTS & EST. 180, 251 (1961). Professor Bogert reached the same conclusion. BOGERT, THE LAW OF TRUSTS AND TRUSTEES § 847 (2d ed. 1962).
160. *In re Gardner's Trust,* 266 Minn. 127, 123 N.W.2d 69 (1963); *In re Arens,* 41 N.J. 364, 197 A.2d 1 (1963); *Catherwood Trust,* 405 Pa. 61, 173 A.2d 86 (1961), *overruling Crawford Est.,* 362 Pa. 458, 67 A.2d 124 (1949). *But cf. Franklin v. Margay Oil Corp.,* 194 Okla. 519, 153 P.2d 486 (1944) (an Oklahoma statute regulating allocation of oil royalties could not constitutionally be applied retroactively).
161. *In re Gardner's Trust,* 266 Minn. 127, 132, 123 N.W.2d 69, 73 (1963).
162. U.S. PRESIDENT'S COMMITTEE ON EDUCATION BEYOND THE HIGH SCHOOL, SECOND REPORT TO THE PRESIDENT 79 (1957); *Report of the Treasurer, 1965-66,* BULL. OF YALE U. 9 (Dec. 15, 1966).
163. *E.g.,* W. VA. CODE ANN. § 44-6-2a (1966).
164. *E.g.,* ILL. ANN. STAT. ch. 32 § 163a 4(f), (h) (Smith-Hurd 1954); TEX. REV. CIV. STAT. ANN. art. 1396-2.02(a)(7), (9) (1962).
165. *E.g.,* ALA. CODE tit. 58 § 47 (1960); KAN. STAT. ANN. § 17-5004 (1964), *as amended* (Supp. 1967); N.C. GEN. STAT. § 36-1 to § 36-3 (1950).
166. N.Y. EDUC. LAW § 226(6) (McKinney 1953).
167. N.Y. MEMBERSHIP CORPS. LAW § 27 (McKinney 1941), *as amended* (Supp. 1968).
168. N.Y. ESTATES, POWERS & TRUSTS LAW § 11-2.2(a)(1)(0) (McKinney 1967).
169. N.Y. ESTATES, POWERS & TRUSTS LAW §§ 11-1.1(a)(2) and 11-1.1(a)(3) (McKinney 1967).
170. CAL. CORP. CODE § 10206(d) (West 1955).
171. PA. STAT. ANN. tit. 15 § 7306 (1967); TENN. CODE ANN. § 48-1108 (1964).
172. MODEL NON-PROFIT CORPORATION ACT § 5(g) (rev. act 1964); ALA. CODE tit. 10 § 207(g) (1960); D.C. CODE ENCYCL. ANN. § 29-1005(g) (1968); NEB. REV. STAT. § 21-1904 (7) (1962); N.C. GEN. STAT. § 55A-15(b)(3) (1965); N.D. CENT. CODE § 10-24-05(7) (1960); ORE. REV. STAT. § 61.061(7) (1953); TEX. REV. CIV. STAT. ANN. art. 1396-2.02(A)(7) (1962); VA. CODE ANN. § 13.1-205(g) (1964); WIS. STAT. ANN. § 181.04(6) (1957). *See also* ILL. ANN. STAT. ch. 32, § 163a4(f) (Smith-Hurd 1954); MO. ANN. STAT. § 355.090(7) (1966).
173. W. VA. CODE ANN. § 44-6-2a (1966). The rule was first articulated in the famous case of *Harvard Col. v. Amory,* 26 Mass. 446, 461 (1830).
174. 4 SCOTT, LAW OF TRUSTS § 389 (3d ed. 1967); FREMONT-SMITH, FOUNDATIONS AND GOVERNMENT 144, 155 (1965); Comment, *The Modern Philanthropic Foundation: A Critique and a Proposal,* 59 YALE L.J. 477, 483 n.49 (1950).
175. BOGERT, THE LAW OF TRUSTS AND TRUSTEES § 612 (2d ed. 1960).
176. *Id.* at § 679; 3 SCOTT, LAW OF TRUSTS § 227.5 (3d ed. 1967).
177. RESTATEMENT (SECOND) OF TRUSTS § 389, comment b (1959).
178. *Yap v. Wah Yen Ki Tuk Tsen Nin Hue of Honolulu,* 43 Hawaii 37 (1958); *Freeman v. Norwalk Cemetery Ass'n,* 88 Ohio App. 446, 100 N.E.2d 267 (1950); 1954 OP. ATT'Y GEN. 150 (N.Y.).
179. W. VA. CODE ANN. § 44-6-2a (1966).
180. Breen, *Legal Aspects of Substituting Common Stocks for Fixed Income Securities Under the Prudent Man Rule,* 159 N.Y.L.J., no. 125, p. 4, col. 1 (June 27, 1968).
181. *Ibid.*
182. *E.g.,* MICH. COMP. LAWS ANN. § 450.126 (1967); N.Y. GEN. CORP. LAW § 60 (McKinney 1943); VT. STAT. ANN. tit. 11 § 104 (1959), *as amended* (Supp. 1967).

71

183. *Compare* 1 HORNSTEIN, CORPORATION LAW AND PRACTICE § 446 (1959), *with* RESTATEMENT (SECOND) OF TRUSTS § 174 (1959).
184. *Smith v. Brown-Borhek Co.,* 414 Pa. 325, 332, 200 A.2d 398, 401 (1964).
185. See 1 HORNSTEIN, *supra* note 183, at § 446.
186. RESTATEMENT (SECOND) OF TRUSTS § 174, comment a (1959).
187. Breen, *Legal Aspects of Substituting Common Stocks for Fixed Income Securities Under the Prudent Man Rule,* 159 N.Y.L.J., no. 126, p. 4, col. 1 (June 28, 1968).
188. 1 HORNSTEIN, *supra* note 183, at § 446.
189. BALLANTINE, CORPORATIONS § 63(a) (rev. ed. 1946).
190. Bishop, *Sitting Ducks and Decoy Ducks: New Trends in the Indemnification of Corporate Directors and Officers,* 77 YALE L.J. 1078, 1101 (1968).
191. OLECK, NON-PROFIT CORPORATIONS, ORGANIZATIONS, AND ASSOCIATIONS § 159 (2d ed. 1965); Chidlaw, *Non-Profit and Charitable Corporations in Colorado,* 36 U. COLO. L. REV. 9, 34 (1963); Taylor, *A New Chapter in the New York Law of Charitable Corporations,* 25 CORNELL L.Q. 382, 398 (1940).
192. *Creighton Home v. Waltman,* 140 Neb. 3, 14, 299 N.W. 261, 264 (1941).
193. *Attorney Gen. v. Olson,* 346 Mass. 190, 198, 191 N.E.2d 132, 137 (1963).
194. Lesher, *The Non-Profit Corporation—A Neglected Stepchild Comes of Age,* 22 BUS. LAW. 951, 969 (1967); Comment, 26 S. CAL. L. REV. 80, 85 (1952).
195. *Ray v. Homewood Hosp.,* 223 Minn. 440, 444, 27 N.W.2d 409, 411 (1947); *see* 1951 OP. ATT'Y GEN. 159 (N.Y.); Pasley, *Non-Profit Corporations—Accountability of Directors and Officers,* 21 BUS. LAW. 621 (1966); Note, 64 HARV. L. REV. 1168, 1174-75 (1951).
196. *Pepperdine Fnd. v. Pepperdine,* 126 Cal. App. 2d 154, 159, 271 P.2d 600, 604 (1954).
197. *Graham Bros. Co. v. Galloway Woman's Col.,* 190 Ark. 692, 699, 81 S.W.2d 837, 840 (1935).
198. *Beard v. Achenbach Mem. Hosp. Ass'n,* 170 F.2d 859, 862 (10th Cir. 1948).
199. Welles, *University Endowments: Revolution Comes to the Ivory Tower,* 1 INSTITUTIONAL INVESTOR, Sept. 1967, at 11.
200. *Report of the Treasurer, 1966-67, BULL. OF YALE U.* 22-23 (Jan. 27, 1968).
201. Welles, *supra* note 199.
202. RESTATEMENT (SECOND) OF TRUSTS §§ 171, 379 (1959).
203. *Id.* § 171, comment h, d.
204. MODEL BUS. CORP. ACT. ANN. § 38 (1960), *as amended* (Supp. 1966).
205. 2 W. FLETCHER, PRIVATE CORPORATIONS § 495 (rev. vol. M. Wolf 1954).
206. 3 *id.* § 1096.
207. MODEL NON-PROFIT CORPORATION ACT § 17 (rev. act 1964).
208. *Id.* § 21.
209. *See, e.g.,* ALA. CODE tit. 10, ch. 9, § 223 (1960); ILL. ANN. STAT. 32 § 163a 20 (1954), *as amended* (1959); IND. STAT. ANN. ch. 6, § 25-516 (1960); MD. CODE ANN. art. 23 § 59 (1966); MO. STAT. ANN. § 355.155 (1966); NEB. REV. STAT. § 21-1920 (1962); TENN. CODE ANN. § 48-1108 (1964); TEX. REV. CIV. STAT. ANN. art. 1396-2.18 (1962), *as amended* (1967).
210. RESTATEMENT (SECOND) OF TRUSTS § 379, comment b (1959).
211. Note, 64 HARV. L. REV. 1168, 1175 (1951); *Report of the Treasurer, supra* note 200.
212. 2 SCOTT, LAW OF TRUSTS § 171.4 (3d ed. 1967).
213. *Massachusetts Charitable Mechanic Ass'n v. Beede,* 320 Mass. 601, 611, 70 N.E.2d 825, 831 (1947).
214. *Wilstach Est.,* 1 Pa. D. & C.2d 197, 213 (Orphan's Ct. 1954).
215. *Id.* at 214.
216. *Graham Bros. Co. v. Galloway Woman's Col.,* 190 Ark. 692, 81 S.W.2d 837 (1935).
217. *Murdoch v. Elliot,* 77 Conn. 247, 58 A. 718 (Sup. Ct. Err. 1904).
218. *Ray v. Homewood Hosp.,* 223 Minn. 440, 27 N.W.2d 409 (1947).
219. CAL. CORP. CODE § 10204 (West 1947).
220. S. 956, A. 1690 § 514(a) (N.Y. 1969-1970).
221. RESTATEMENT (SECOND) OF TRUSTS §§ 171, 379 (1959).
222. Investment Company Act of 1940, 15 U.S.C. § 80a-15(a)(3) (1963).

Appendix

Although they are not directly germane to the subject matter of our report, we present here for those interested a short analysis of cases in which charitable corporations have been said to hold their property "absolutely" or "in trust," when the issue presented has not involved administration as such.

The first broad category of such cases consists of those in which the charitable corporation and some other claimant vie for possession of a fund, or the title of the charitable corporation to its property is otherwise put in question (as in a suit for specific performance of a contract for the sale of real estate). The charity prevails far more often than not. Quite often these cases involve testamentary gifts to charitable corporations which are contested by the heirs or residuary legatees of the decedent, who argue that the gift involves a trust which is void under the law of the jurisdiction in question, or that the corporation lacks legal power to act as a trustee. Such arguments are usually resolved in favor of the charity by a holding that the gift was outright and not in trust.[1] Conversely, where an estate was insufficient to satisfy all bequests and the decedent had specified that those establishing "trust funds" should be favored, a Massachusetts court experienced no difficulty in transforming seemingly outright gifts to charitable corporations into trust funds.[2]

New York courts, as the leading exponents of the absolute ownership doctrine, uniformly construe simple bequests to charitable corporations as outright and not in trust.[3] But unincorporated charitable associations, unlike corporations, cannot in New York hold the legal title to property, and outright gifts to them would therefore fail. The New York courts solve this dilemma by construing simple bequests to unincorporated associations as gifts in trust, even though identical language in a bequest to a charitable corporation would be held to describe an absolute gift.[4] Far from being embarrassed by the apparent discrepancy, the courts seem not even to have noticed it.

The converse arises in New Jersey, the leading exponent of the trust theory, where the courts on several occasions have gone out of their way to construe simple bequests of personalty to unincorporated charitable associations as outright and not in trust.[5] In the circumstances of the particular cases, such a construction preserved the gifts for charity and had the additional advantage of doing away with the necessity of finding some continuing entity to administer the gift.*

California courts have chosen whichever of the two theories was of most help in sustaining the particular charitable gift then under consideration. A deed to named individuals as trustees for an unincorporated charitable association was attacked as a trust void for vagueness. The court sustained the conveyance by holding that it was absolute and not in trust, despite the fact that the association's lack of legal capacity required the individuals to hold the legal title.[7] A later case considered a bequest to an unincorporated charitable association, which the testator's heirs attacked as an outright gift to an association which lacked power to take it. This time the court upheld the gift by construing it as one to the trustees of the association, "in trust to carry out the objects for which the organization was created."[8]**

From time to time the members of charitable corporations have attempted to dissolve their organizations and distribute the assets among themselves. The courts have been quick to block such attempts, usually upon the rationale that the funds are impressed with a "public trust" and cannot be diverted to private uses.[12]

Charitable corporations have on occasion experienced financial reverses and been unable to meet their debts. When their creditors have sued, the courts have often barred recovery on the ground that the funds of the corporations are held in trust for charity.[13] The same "trust fund"

---

*It should be noted, however, that where the bequest to an unincorporated association imposes restrictions on the use or administration of the fund, New Jersey courts will appoint a trustee.[6]

**Examples abound of the ambivalent approach of the courts to cases in this area. Regardless of the jurisdiction the noncharity claimant will find the scales of justice heavily weighted against him. Three cases from Indiana further illustrate the point. In the first a testator had left his residuary estate in equal parts to a hospital for the treatment of poor persons and to a church for the installation of chimes (with any balance to be applied to the general purposes of the church). His heirs attacked the bequests as invalid trusts, but the court held that "in a case where property is given directly to a charitable institution for the purpose of promoting some or all of its general charitable purposes it is not a trust in the same sense as an ordinary private trust."[9] In the second case, decided subsequently, a testatrix left the remainder of her estate to a Bible Institute "to be used in the publication and dissemination of evangelical Christian literature in harmony with its Articles of Incorporation." Prior to her death the institute had merged with a similar institution. The heirs of the testatrix argued that the bequest was absolute and had lapsed. The court sustained it, saying that the specification by the testatrix of the purpose for which it could be used made it clear that it was in trust.[10] In the third case the residuary legatees of a testatrix argued that her bequest to a foreign missionary society "to be used for China, India and Africa" was void because it attempted to establish an invalid trust. The court preserved this gift for charity also, this time by holding that the bequest was absolute and not in trust.[11]

theory underlies the doctrine that eleemosynary institutions are immune from liability for the torts of their agents.[14] The justice of such holdings may well be questioned, and in fact they are becoming increasingly rare,[15] but they demonstrate the tendency of most courts to favor charities in disputes involving claims to money or property. This observation is underscored by the fact that the "trust fund" theory of tort immunity was adopted in several states which wholeheartedly espoused the doctrine of absolute ownership for other purposes.[16]

On occasion a testator bequeaths property to a charitable corporation which is to be formed at some time in the future. The courts generally construe such a bequest as a charitable trust in order to prevent the gift from failing for lack of a legal entity to hold the title.[17] For the same reason there is a similar tendency to find a charitable trust where the charitable corporation which has been designated by the testator to receive the bequest is non-existent or refuses the gift.[18]* In a few states it is still necessary to find a trust to exist before the courts can apply the doctrine of cy pres,[23] but in most jurisdictions the doctrine can now be applied to preserve gifts for charity whether or not the intended charitable recipient is deemed to hold its property in trust.[24]

From the foregoing it can be seen that courts will go to great lengths to preserve property for charity when a charitable corporation's title is disputed by a private person. Trust principles or corporate principles are applied primarily for their assistance in rationalizing the desired conclusion, and inconsistencies in such application are brushed aside or ignored. Where monetary considerations are not involved, however, the picture is less clear.

---

*An extreme example arose in California, where a testatrix established a trust for the benefit of a life beneficiary, on the death of whom *"this trust shall cease and terminate,* and all of the trust estate . . . shall be distributed and paid [to named charities] . . . *free from any trust."*[19] One of the charities refused the bequest. In order to apply cy pres and save the gift for charity the court had to find a trust, and it therefore reached the rather remarkable conclusion that "it is inescapable that the intent of the testatrix . . . was to create charitable trusts."[20]

Two New York cases are of interest in this connection. In one a testator had bequeathed the remainder interest in a testamentary trust to a number of charitable corporations, one of which became bankrupt after the testator's death but before the death of the life tenant. The other charitable corporations sought to invoke cy pres in order that they might divide the bankrupt's share, while the testator's next of kin argued (erroneously, it should be noted) that cy pres was inapplicable because of the absence of a trust. The court preserved the bankrupt's share for the remaining charitable corporations by holding that "Every gift to a charitable corporation for a charitable purpose involves a trust in the real sense of the word."[21] In the second case a charitable corporation was to take the remainder interest in a testamentary trust for the support of a specified activity, which it discontinued shortly after the life beneficiary's death but before distribution to it of the estate. Here, unlike the first case, the testator had provided for a non-charitable disposition of "lapsed" legacies. The court preserved the gift for charity by holding that the trust terminated on the death of the life tenant and vested absolutely in the charitable corporation; therefore, there could be no "lapse" when the specified activity was subsequently discontinued. The court then applied the doctrine of cy pres to require the charitable corporation to use the bequest for a purpose similar to that of the discontinued activity.[22]

Suits to enforce restrictions imposed by the donors of gifts to charitable corporations have been productive of a number of judicial decisions dealing with the trust—absolute ownership dichotomy.* At one time there was a reluctance in "absolute ownership" states to hold that the donor had meant to impose enforceable restrictions, because at that time such a holding would have been tantamount to finding an invalid trust. Therefore, to save the gifts for charity, the courts brushed many such restrictions aside as "precatory."[33] In "trust theory" states, conversely, courts wishing to uphold restrictions tended to employ trust language.[34] Today courts everywhere enforce restrictions regardless of whether the charitable corporation holds its funds outright or in trust.[35]**

A similar line of cases deals with the application of cy pres. Here the corporation itself is often the plaintiff, seeking permission of the court to apply its funds to a use different from that specified by the donor, or to expend principal which the donor required to be maintained intact. The doctrine of cy pres was conceived in the womb of trust law, and courts applying the doctrine naturally tend to employ trust language.[37] Other courts wishing to grant the relief sought sometimes hold that the corporation owns its property outright and, within the limits of its corporate charter, can deal with such property as it sees fit.[38] Today courts in most states apply cy pres, either by statute or by judicial decision, regardless of the character of the corporation's property interest,[39] and discussions of the absolute ownership-trust dichotomy in such cases are therefore somewhat anachronistic.

Occasionally donations have been accepted by charitable corporations with the understanding that they are to constitute the endowment

---

*It is customary to state that only the attorney general has standing to bring such a suit,[25] and a number of cases have so held,[26] but cases can nevertheless be cited in nearly every jurisdiction in which such complaints were entertained from a donor[27] or his heirs[28] or from a member of the corporation[29] or a taxpayer[30] or a disgruntled public official.[31] This is not necessarily an unhealthy situation, because the understaffed and overworked offices of most state attorneys general are simply incapable of doing an effective job of monitoring the activities of all of the charities under their ostensible supervision.[32]

**But if the restrictions are such that they would render the property worthless or substantially less useful, or would threaten the charity's title to the property, the courts tend to ignore them (or, when the remedy is available, to grant relief through cy pres). An interesting example arose in Maryland, where a childrens' home was bequeathed a remainder interest in a testamentary trust to be used as an endowment fund, with the income to provide free treatment in the diphtheria and scarlet fever wards. When the will was drafted diphtheria and scarlet fever were dread diseases; when the life tenant died thirty years thereafter they were much less prevalent and virulent and ward treatment of contagious diseases was considered poor practice. The home brought a construction proceeding, asking that it not be restricted to the purposes mentioned in the will because that "would involve waste and impair the fulfillment of the testatrix's general intention."[36] Cy pres was unavailable, because the will had been drafted prior to the enactment of legislation establishing the doctrine in Maryland. The court held that the trust had terminated at the death of the life tenant and that the charity was therefore free to ignore the restriction. The principal of the fund was ordered to be held intact and only the income spent. The court did not note the apparent inconsistency of ignoring one restriction and enforcing another (the preservation of principal).

for a certain number of scholarships or hospital beds. With the passage of time rising costs have made such agreements unprofitable for the charities and they have turned to the courts for relief. Some courts have applied contract principles and held the charitable corporation to its bargain.[40] Others have applied cy pres to allow the corporation to charge for the portion of its costs not covered by the income from the endowment.[41]

Quarrels between two warring factions of a church, squabbling over ownership of the church's property, have been another fertile source of decisions in this area. The courts in such situations are asked to decide whether the local incorporated church holds its property "in trust" for the local congregation; the cases go both ways.[42] Those cases which hold that incorporated churches are trustees for their local congregations are themselves split over whether the "true" congregation is that faction which consists of a majority of current members, or that faction whose members adhere most closely to the original tenets of the church or the teachings of a national body or synod.[43] None of these cases is close enough to our factual situation to be of any practical use in solving the problems with which we are concerned. The "trust" which these decisions debate is quite a different animal from the financial trust which might mandate the classification of capital gains as principal.

Other non-administration cases include a small number which discuss the applicability of various taxes or assessments to charitable corporations, in their capacity as owners or trustees of property. These cases are too diverse and too few in number to be helpful in the present discussion.[44]

Also in the non-administration category are two New Jersey cases, in which some enterprising purveyors of tombstones sued to enjoin public cemetery corporations from competing with them, on the theory that it was unseemly and ultra vires for "charitable trusts" such as the cemeteries to engage in a business for profit. The plaintiffs prevailed.[45]

Notes to Appendix

1. *Zabel v. Stewart*, 153 Kan. 272, 109 P.2d 177 (1941); *Whitmore v. Congregational Parish*, 121 Me. 391, 117 A. 469 (1922); *Lane v. Eaton*, 69 Minn. 141, 71 N.W. 1031 (1897); *National Bd. v. Fry*, 293 Mo. 399, 239 S.W. 519 (1922).
2. *Smith v. Livermore*, 298 Mass. 223, 10 N.E.2d 117 (1937).
3. *St. Joseph's Hosp. v. Bennett*, 281 N.Y. 115, 22 N.E.2d 305 (1939); *Robert v. Corning*, 89 N.Y. 225 (1882); *Wetmore v. Parker*, 52 N.Y. 450 (1873); *In re Arrowsmith*, 162 App. Div. 623, 147 N.Y.S. 1016 (1st Dep't 1914), *aff'd mem.*, 213 N.Y. 704, 108 N.E. 1089 (1915); *Brayton v. Rector, etc., of Christ Church*, 249 App. Div. 290, 292 N.Y.S. 131 (4th Dep't 1936), *aff'd mem.*, 275 N.Y. 631, 11 N.E.2d 792 (1937); *In re Teed*, 59 Hun. 63, 12 N.Y.S. 642 (5th Dep't 1891); *In re Will of Pelton*, 190 Misc. 624, 74 N.Y.S.2d 743 (Sur. Ct. 1947); *In re Fowler's Est.*, 43 N.Y.S.2d 94 (Sur. Ct. 1943), *aff'd mem.*, 268 App. Div. 788, 50 N.Y.S.2d 174 (2d Dep't), *motion for leave to appeal denied*, 293 N.Y. 934, 57 N.E.2d 752 (1944); *In re Colgate*, 165 Misc. 251, 300 N.Y.S. 940 (Sur. Ct. 1937); *In re Arber*, 151 Misc. 861, 272 N.Y.S. 684 (Sur. Ct. 1934); *In re Roche*, 53 Misc. 187, 104 N.Y.S. 601 (Sur. Ct. 1907); *see* 1951 OP. ATT'Y GEN. 159, 160 (N.Y.).
4. *In re Est. of Winburn*, 139 Misc. 5, 247 N.Y.S. 584 (Sur. Ct. 1931).
5. *New Jersey Title Guar. & Trust Co. v. American Nat'l Red Cross*, 111 N.J. Eq. 12, 160 A. 842 (Ch. 1932); *Hadden v. Dandy*, 51 N.J. Eq. 154, 26 A. 464 (Ch.), *aff'd*, 51 N.J. Eq. 330, 30 A. 429 (E. & A. 1893).
6. *Bruere v. Cook*, 63 N.J. Eq. 624, 52 A. 1001 (Ch. 1902), *aff'd mem.*, 67 N.J. Eq. 724, 63 A. 1118 (E. & A. 1903); *Mason's Ex'rs v. Trustees of the Methodist Episcopal Church*, 27 N.J. Eq. 47 (Ch. 1876). *See also White v. Mayor & Common Council*, 89 N.J. Eq. 5, 103 A. 1042 (Ch. 1918).
7. *Brittenbaker v. Buck*, 58 Cal. App. 738, 209 P. 264 (1st Dist. 1922).
8. *Estate of McDole*, 215 Cal. 328, 334, 10 P.2d 75, 77 (1932).
9. *Crawfordsville Trust Co. v. Elston Bank & Trust Co.*, 216 Ind. 596, 610, 25 N.E.2d 626, 631 (1940).
10. *Bible Inst. Colportage Ass'n v. St. Joseph's B. & T. Co.*, 118 Ind. App. 592, 75 N.E.2d 666 (1947).
11. *Stockton v. Northwestern Branch Missionary Soc'y*, 127 Ind. App. 193, 133 N.E.2d 875 (1956).
12. *In re Los Angeles Pioneer Soc'y*, 40 Cal.2d 852, 257 P.2d 1, *cert. den.*, 346 U.S. 888 (1953); *Ashton v. Dashaway Ass'n*, 84 Cal. 61, 22 P. 660, *aff'd mem. in banc*, 23 P. 1091 (1890); *Sherman v. Richmond Hose Co. No. 2*, 230 N.Y. 462, 130 N.E. 613 (1921); *Commonwealth v. Pauline Home*, 141 Pa. 537, 21 A. 661 (1891); *Humane Fire Co.'s Appeal*, 88 Pa. 389 (1879); *Mayer v. Society*, 2 Brewst. 385 (Pa. Sup. Ct. 1868); *Thomas v. Ellmaker*, 1 Pars. 98 (Pa. Ct. C.P. 1844); *accord, Lynch v. Spilman*, 67 Cal. 2d 247, 431 P.2d 636, 62 Cal. Rptr. 12 (1967). *But see Cone v. Wold*, 85 Minn. 302, 88 N.W. 977 (1902) (donations held on a resulting trust in favor of the donors).
13. *Hobbs v. Board of Ed.*, 126 Neb. 416, 253 N.W. 627 (1934); *Crane v. Morristown School Fnd.*, 120 N.J. Eq. 583, 187 A. 632 (E. & A. 1936); *Mills v. Davison*, 54 N.J. Eq. 659, 35 A. 1072 (E. & A. 1896).
14. *See, e.g., Fordyce v. Woman's Christian Nat'l Library Ass'n*, 79 Ark. 550, 96 S.W. 155 (1906); *St. Mary's Academy v. Solomon*, 77 Colo. 463, 238 P. 22 (1925).
15. *See, e.g., Parker v. Port Huron Hosp.*, 361 Mich. 1, 105 N.W.2d 1 (1960), *overruling Downes v. Harper Hosp.*, 101 Mich. 555, 60 N.W. 42 (1894). *See also* CHAMBERS, COLLEGES AND THE COURTS: 1936-40, 91 (1941).
16. *Loeffler v. Sheppard-Pratt Hosp.*, 130 Md. 265, 100 A. 301 (1917); *Perry v. House of Refuge*, 63 Md. 20 (1885); *Downes v. Harper Hosp.*, 101 Mich. 555, 60 N.W. 42 (1894) (deeds in trust to found hospital), *overruled, Parker v. Port Huron Hosp.*, 361 Mich. 1, 105 N.W.2d 1 (1960).
17. *Franklin v. Hastings*, 253 Ill. 46, 97 N.E. 265 (1912); *accord, Jansen v. Godair*, 292 Ill. 364, 127 N.E. 97 (1920); *Crerar v. Williams*, 145 Ill. 625, 34 N.E. 467 (1893).
18. *Richardson v. Mullery*, 200 Mass. 247, 86 N.E. 319 (1908); *Howard Savings Institute v. Peep*, 34 N.J. 494, 170 A.2d 39 (1960) (gift "in trust"); *Bowman v. Domestic & Foreign Missionary Soc'y*, 182 N.Y. 494, 75 N.E. 535 (1905); *Mears' Est.*, 299 Pa. 217, 149 A. 157 (1930).
19. *Estate of Faulkner*, 128 Cal. App. 2d 575, 577-78, 275 P.2d 818, 820 (1st Dist. 1954) (emphasis altered).

20. *Id.* at 578, 275 P.2d at 820.
21. *In re Brundrett's Est.*, 87 N.Y.S.2d 851, 852 (Sur. Ct. 1940).
22. *In re Lee's Will*, 3 Misc.2d 1072, 156 N.Y.S.2d 813 (Sup. Ct. 1956).
23. *E.g., Stockton v. Northwestern Branch Missionary Soc'y*, 127 Ind. App. 193, 133 N.E.2d 875 (1956); *In re Lowe's Est.*, 117 Ind. App. 554, 70 N.E.2d 187 (1946).
24. *E.g., Wilson Est.*, 63 Montg. Co. L.R. 112 (Pa. Orphans' Ct. 1947); RESTATEMENT (SECOND) OF TRUSTS § 348, comment f (1959); Scott, *Charitable Trusts in New York*, 26 N.Y.U. L.REV. 251, 259 (1959).
25. *E.g., Judkins v. Hyannis Public Library Ass'n*, 302 Mass. 425, 19 N.E.2d 727 (1939); Bogert, *Proposed Legislation Regarding State Supervision of Charities*, 52 MICH. L. REV. 633, 633-34 (1954).
26. *E.g., Holden Hosp. Corp. v. Southern Ill. Hosp. Corp.*, 22 Ill. 2d 150, 174 N.E.2d 793 (1961); *Voelker v. St. Louis Mercantile Library Ass'n*, 359 S.W.2d 689 (Mo. Sup. Ct. 1962); *Cadman Memorial Congreg. Soc'y v. Kenyon*, 306 N.Y. 151, 116 N.E.2d 481 (1953).
27. *E.g., Associate Alumni v. Theological Seminary*, 163 N.Y. 417, 57 N.E. 626 (1900); *Packard v. Thiel Col.*, 207 Pa. 280, 56 A. 869 (1903).
28. *E.g., Lovelace v. Marion Inst.*, 215 Ala. 271, 110 So. 381 (1926); *Catron v. Scarritt Collegiate Inst.*, 264 Mo. 713, 175 S.W. 571 (1915); *Loechel v. Columbia Borough School Dist.*, 369 Pa. 132, 85 A.2d 81 (1952); *Glatfelter v. School Dist.*, 52 Lanc. L. Rev. 325 (Pa. 1951).
29. *E.g., Ashton v. Dashaway Ass'n*, 84 Cal. 61, 22 P. 660, aff'd *mem. in banc*, 23 P. 1091 (1890); *Denckla v. Independence Fnd.*, 41 Del. Ch. 247, 193 A.2d 538 (Sup. Ct. 1963); *Mayer v. Society*, 2 Brewst. 385 (Pa. Sup. Ct. 1868).
30. *E.g., Hermosa Beach v. Superior Ct.*, 231 Cal. App. 2d 295, 41 Cal. Rptr. 796 (2d Dist. 1964); *Tash v. Ludden*, 88 Neb. 292, 129 N.W. 417 (1911); *cf. Board of Mayor & Aldermen v. Wilson*, 232 Miss. 435, 99 So.2d 674 (1958).
31. *E.g., Aurora v. Y.M.C.A.*, 9 Ill. 2d 286, 137 N.E.2d 347 (1956).
32. *Paterson v. Paterson Gen. Hosp.*, 97 N.J. Super. 514, 235 A.2d 487 (Ch. 1967); FREMONT-SMITH, FOUNDATIONS AND GOVERNMENT 234-41 (1965); Karst, *The Efficiency of the Charitable Dollar: An Unfulfilled State Responsibility*, 73 HARV. L. REV. 433 (1960).
33. *E.g., Corporation of the Chamber of Commerce v. Bennett*, 143 Misc. 513, 257 N.Y.S. 2 (Sup. Ct. 1932).
34. *E.g., Montclair Nat'l Bank & Trust Co. v. Seton Hall Col. of Med.*, 90 N.J. Super. 419, 217 A.2d 897 (Ch. 1966).
35. *E.g., Lyme High School Ass'n v. Alling*, 113 Conn. 200, 154 A. 439 (1931); *Trustees of Peninsula Ann. Conf. v. New York East Ann. Conf.*, 211 A.2d 588 (Del. Ch. 1965); *Hanover St. Presbyterian Church v. Buckson*, 210 A.2d 190 (Del. Ch. 1965); *Newhall v. Second Church & Soc'y*, 349 Mass. 493, 209 N.E.2d 296 (1965); *St. Joseph's Hosp. v. Bennett*, 281 N.Y. 115, 22 N.E.2d 305 (1939); *Estate of Berry*, 29 Wis. 2d 506, 139 N.W.2d 72 (1966).
36. *Gray v. Harriet Lane Home*, 192 Md. 251, 258, 64 A.2d 102, 105 (1949).
37. *Knights of Equity v. University of Detroit*, 359 Mich. 235, 102 N.W.2d 463 (1960); *In re Y.M.C.A. War Fund*, 63 Ohio App. 213, 25 N.E.2d 956 (1939).
38. *Loomis Inst. v. Healy*, 98 Conn. 102, 119 A. 31 (1922); *Gray v. Harriet Lane Home*, 192 Md. 251, 64 A.2d 102 (1949).
39. *Trevathan v. Ringgold-Nolan Fnd.*, 241 Ark. 758, 410 S.W.2d 132 (1967); *Estate of Berry*, 29 Wis. 2d 506, 139 N.W.2d 72 (1966).
40. *Hopkins v. Women's Med. Col.*, 331 Pa. 42, 200 A. 32 (1938); *Alumnae Ass'n of William Penn High School v. University of Pa.*, 306 Pa. 283, 159 A. 449 (1932).
41. *Knights of Equity v. University of Detroit*, 359 Mich. 235, 102 N.W.2d 463 (1960).
42. For cases finding absolute ownership, *see, e.g., Greek Orthodox Community v. Malicourtis*, 267 Mass. 472, 166 N.E. 863 (1929); *McNeilly v. First Presbyterian Church*, 243 Mass. 331, 137 N.E. 691 (1923); *Enos v. Church of St. John the Baptist*, 187 Mass. 40, 72 N.E. 253 (1904); *Warner v. Bowdoin Square Baptist Soc'y*, 148 Mass. 400, 19 N.E. 403 (1889). For cases finding a trust, *see, e.g., Baker v. Ducker*, 79 Cal. 365, 21 P. 764 (1889); *Dubs v. Egli*, 167 Ill. 514, 47 N.E. 766 (1897); *St. Michael's Ukrainian Greek Catholic Church v. St. Michael's Ukrainian Orthodox Church*, 288 Mass. 258, 192 N.E. 628 (1934); *Kelly v. McIntire*, 123 N.J. Eq. 351, 197 A. 736 (Ch. 1938); *Morgan v. Rose*, 22 N.J. Eq. 583 (E. & A. 1871); *Trustees of the Associate Reformed Church v. Trustees of the Theological Seminary*, 4 N.J. Eq. 77 (Ch. 1837); *In re Dissolution of Susquehanna Ave. Presbyterian Church*, 31 Pa. D.&C. 597 (1938); *St. Mary's Russian Orthodox Greek Catholic Church v. Hrieceniak*, 38 Lack. Jur. 129 (Pa. 1936); *Schnorr's Appeal*, 67 Pa. 138 (1870).
43. Majority rule governed in *Dubs v. Egli*, 167 Ill. 514, 47 N.E. 766 (1897); *St. Michael's Ukrainian Greek Catholic Church v. St. Michael's Ukrainian Orthodox Church*, 288 Mass. 258, 192 N.E. 628 (1934). The faction with the original tenets took the property in *Baker v. Ducker*, 79 Cal. 365, 21 P. 764 (1889); *Kelly v. McIntire*, 123 N.J. Eq. 351, 197 A. 736 (Ch. 1938); *Trustees of the Associate Reformed Church v. Trustees of the Theological Seminary*, 4 N.J. Eq. 77 (Ch. 1837); *In re Dissolution of Susquehanna Ave. Presbyterian Church*, 31 Pa. D.&C. 597 (1938); *St. Mary's Russian Orthodox Greek Catholic Church*

v. Hrieceniak, 38 Lack. Jur. 129 (Pa. 1936); *Schnorr's Appeal*, 67 Pa. 138 (1870).

44. *Pacific Home v. Los Angeles*, 41 Cal. 2d 844, 264 P.2d 539 (1953); *Monticello Seminary v. Board of Review*, 249 Ill. 481, 94 N.E. 938 (1911); *Gamble v. Cumberland Col.*, 4 F. Supp. 767 (E.D. Ky. 1933); *Wellesley Col. v. Attorney Gen.*, 313 Mass. 722, 49 N.E.2d 220 (1943); *Animal Rescue League v. Assessors*, 310 Mass. 330, 37 N.E.2d 1019 (1941); *O'Brien v. Physicians Hosp. Ass'n*, 96 Ohio St. 1, 116 N.E. 975 (1917); *William Budge Memorial Hosp. v. Maughan*, 79 Utah 516, 3 P.2d 258 (1931).

45. *Terwilliger v. Graceland Memorial Park Ass'n*, 35 N.J. 259, 173 A.2d 33 (1961); *Frank v. Clover Leaf Park Cemetery Ass'n*, 29 N.J. 193, 148 A.2d 488 (1959).